THE BUSINESS SECRETS OF DRUG DEALING

T0021013

MATT TAIBBI
AND REGGIE HARRIS

THE BUSINESS SECRETS OF DRUGDEALING

AN ALMOST TRUE ACCOUNT

OR Books

New York · London

Published by OR Books, New York and London
Visit our website at www.orbooks.com

All rights information: rights@orbooks.com

First printing 2022

Cataloging-in-Publication data is available from the Library of Congress.
A catalog record for this book is available from the British Library.

Typeset by Lapiz Digital Services. Printed by BookMobile, USA, and CPI, UK.

paperback ISBN 978-1-68219-341-9 • ebook ISBN 978-1-68219-342-6

AUTHORS' NOTE

This is a work of fiction, inspired by truth.

In real life, there is a person like Huey Carmichael. He keeps
rules. The real Huey knows more than a thing or two about the
weed business. The part about him always having a square job
is also true. There are some employers who would be shocked
to learn that one of their own had a hobby this extensive. Huey
is out of the game now.

Many of the observations and thoughts described here are
real. Everything else is fictionalized. We wanted to preserve
Huey's voice and point of view without delving too deeply into
real events. Any resemblance to real people in this story is
coincidental.

—Matt Taibbi and Reggie Harris

PREFACE

You gotta have a code.

There has to be stuff you won't do. Like: I won't sell anything that doesn't grow out of the ground. If you make it in a lab or a trailer that might explode, I don't want shit to do with it.

Most dealers, no joke, learn their jobs from movies. They watch and re-watch *Paid in Full* or *Blow* or *The Wire* or *New Jack City* or a half-dozen other films. Now with Netflix there are more, from *Ozark* to *Justified* to *Narcos*. There's some influence from music, too, from songs like "Ten Crack Commandments" by Biggie, to others by Berner, Young Dolph, Cyhi the Prince, and even Jay-Z.

But when I was younger, there was almost nothing for guidance. And this bothered me. I thought, "There has to be a better way to learn this game."

So I made it my business to create rules. I kept them all in my head, hundreds of them, and added to and tweaked them over the years.

I'm only writing them down now.

Like: *Get your money and get out.* Time is not on your side. Sooner or later, your run is going to end. You'll be dead or in jail, as the cliché goes.

You have to be perfect 100 percent of the time. The police only have to get lucky once.

They weren't lucky with me.

I got out.

1

Keep your spot to yourself.

As soon as I pull into my driveway, I see Brutus coming.

"Yo, Huey!" he says, starting to cross the street.

Oh, shit. Brutus will talk your fucking head off if you let him.

He's an OG, maybe sixty to sixty-five years old, Blood-affiliated. He's bald, swole, has muscles on muscles, and is terrifying to look at. His body's ripped, with tats crawling up his neck and face, but he walks with a limp.

He's waiting for settlement money after getting hit by a city bus. He's always bitching about it. He thinks his lawyers are fucking him on the deal and always wants to tell you all about it. You can lose an hour if you let him get started.

I step out of my ten-year-old Toyota Corolla, a nothing car you wouldn't notice. That's the point: nobody looks at it twice. The minute I put my first fifty pounds in its trunk, that Toyota paid for itself. I turn around.

"Brutus," I say. "What's up?"

"Nothing, blood, I just haven't seen you. How you been?"

When Brutus talks, every third word out of his mouth is "blood." It's always, "Listen, blood, I'm telling you, blood . . ." A few times I've had to actually cut him off with that. I don't want there to be a misunderstanding, for me to get blessed in by mistake, like I'm a Blood too just by him saying it so many times.

Also, just to make an observation, Brutus does not wear a shirt 100 percent of the time he's out of his house. He's not wearing one now.

"Brutus, man," I say, "I don't mean to be rude, but I just came back for a minute. I don't have time for a conversation. What's going on?"

"You got my text?"

I do have one phone I use, although rarely, and never for business.

Anybody who uses phones, they're going down. Phone tapping is the most basic technique cops use. What they're not on is the encryption. I haven't used phones since Obama's first term. We were using BlackBerries back then.

Having Brutus as a neighbor is a relationship that cuts both ways. He keeps an eye on my place. If he sees anyone creeping around he doesn't recognize, he'll text me. But it took a long time to get him to stop asking for weed on the phone. Now if he wants something, he'll text me an asterisk. Not much of an improvement, but a step in the right direction.

I look at my phone. There, a few days old, is an asterisk.

"Gonna take me a day," I say.

"That's cool, blood, that's cool."

He reaches over and slips fifty in my pocket. I don't look down. The man is older than me, so I don't like to count money in front of him. I don't disrespect him like that. I don't like that power dynamic.

"All right," I say, eyes forward. "Let me get with these white boys. I'll be back tomorrow."

I could give him an ounce right then, but I want him thinking I'm broke, or near it. He thinks I've got a square job—which

I do, I always do, that's one of my rules, *always have a job*—and that I have some white friends I buy from. Close to the truth, but not quite.

In reality, in my house, just a dozen or so yards away, I've got a Tupperware cabinet that's just full of weed. Out in the big, West Coast city where I live, you buy what they call "grower's pounds," and grower's pounds are always over a half an ounce to an ounce.

A traditional East Coast pound is 448 grams. A grower's pound might be 456, something like that. It's a heavy pound. But I just take the extras off all those grower's pounds, and that's what I give to him.

But I wait a day. I let Brutus go back to his house. I let night fall. I go out for a drive in the morning. I come back. I see him, like he often is, on his front steps doing jailhouse push-ups on a diagonal—feet on the sidewalk, hands on the stoop. I let him look up and see me pull into the driveway. He gets up from his porch and limps over again with that same big smile on his face.

Now I hand him the ounce or whatever.

"Yo, blood, thank you, blood, thank you," he says, and starts to cry.

Brutus cries every time I see him, because he gets so emotional about how happy he is that I help him.

"That's all right, Brutus."

"No seriously, Huey, blood—look at me, dog, I'm tearing up."

"It's okay. We'll talk later, all right?"

He waves, still sniffling, and drags his massive body back to his stoop.

And that's every time I come home, too, because Brutus is always home, every single day. He's got shit else to do. He used to sell crack, big time. He went to prison a while back, because he got caught with a couple ounces of it. But he convinced the prosecutor that he was a user and not a seller, so they reduced his time.

Brutus told me once that when he was coming up, his OG told him that it's always better to look like a user than a dealer when caught. That's a lesson I've remembered over the years. White friends when they get caught dealing pull this, and they get rehab. Brutus used it to get a reduced prison sentence.

Brutus has got a past. Armed robberies, home invasions. He's a violent person, in other words, but not violent with me. That can be a good thing if I keep the relationship right. I think he smokes a little crack now. I can't be sure. But he's got teeth missing, and he sometimes just seems obliterated. Not good signs. He's also got a girlfriend who looks pretty good from a distance, but look up close and she's missing a few teeth too. I think she's the one got him smoking.

The only reason I give him weed is so he doesn't starve. He doesn't work, and is on hard times. So I'd rather give him a couple of ounces every month, and have him happy and docile, instead of starving and looking.

I tell all this to illustrate a rule: *Never let business partners know where you stay.*

Brutus is the only person on earth who knows where I live.

There's not much to be done about it. The guy lives across the street. He sees me. So I make the best of it. And again, played right, there are benefits to the relationship.

But nobody else knows. Not family members, not business partners, not girlfriends. Nobody.

I've been to where they all live. But nobody knows where I am.

2

No guns, but keep shooters.

August 1999. I'm seventeen years old. I'm in a shitty little East Coast town called Mountainside, in New Jersey, driving my father's gold Infiniti, with my father's license plates, about to do an armed robbery. There are three other guys in the car, all with stockings on their laps, ready to go.

I'm freaking out. I don't want to do this. I'm already in the business and making good money by then, but some of my old friends from the hood aren't doing so well.

And they know I have a gun. It's a seven-shot Taurus .357 Magnum revolver with a four-inch barrel and hollow tips. It's a massive, fierce-looking gun. Way too much power for a high school kid to have. I shouldn't have it, but I do, and they know it.

That's because I messed around and showed it off. And one day, during summer school, these guys were like, "Man, we're hurting. We really need some help. Come on, man, if you can't set us up at least take us on a lick."

And I'm like, "What's a lick?"

See, I was living in the suburbs by then, and only came home to the West Ward periodically. I didn't even know about shit like this.

"A robbery," says my crazy Jamaican friend Romeo. We call him Ro for short. "Let's do a robbery."

He presses me and I make a bad decision. I figure I'd rather have these old friends thinking I'm with them than to start thinking I'm holding out. They might start to get curious about where I keep my own money. I don't want them robbing me, so I decide to go with them on this job.

So we go, from the Ivy Hill projects out toward Short Hills. There are four of us. I'm behind the wheel. Romeo is in the back with the big silver gun, tapping it on his thigh. Ro is crazy, a thug's thug. There's no tapping out in a fight with him, no telling him to chill. It ends when he says it ends. Think Kimbo Slice in high school. Everyone's afraid of him.

Matter of fact, he's on the run right now. He jumped out of a building in a juvenile detention facility, gotten ghost and run off. He just doesn't give a fuck.

Sitting next to him is a rail-thin light-skinned kid named Terrence who lives in Ro's building. He's into all kinds of shit with him. They're doing elevator robberies together, that kind of thing. Lastly, there's a huge guy named Curtis Ramsey, a two-sport star back in Ivy Hill. He's more my friend than theirs and looks nervous as hell sitting up front with me.

We wait until sundown before setting off on a random trip around the New Jersey suburbs. We have no plan at all. We're driving around with masks in our laps, saying things like, "Where should we go?" "How about here?" "What's a town with a lot of money?"

Finally Ro shouts from the back seat: "Yo, Huey, how about we try *your* neighborhood?"

I don't like that very much, but we do it. The problem is, Short Hills gets pretty slow after dark. We roll through some residential neighborhoods and there are literally no people on the sidewalks, no one in driveways.

"Ro, man, there's no one here. I live near a golf course, you understand? It's dark out."

"Let's go up another block," Ro says.

"I'm telling you, there's no one here."

"Take a left."

We keep driving. It's getting late. Finally, to my relief, Ro gives up on Short Hills. We drive around for a while and end up in what I think is a crappy little suburb called Mountainside. There are a few people out and about, on account of there's a big movie theater there maybe.

I keep thinking: I don't like this. This isn't my game. In the rearview mirror I can see Ro looking anxious as we turn into a residential area. Over and over, we'd see someone and he'd tell me to stop. "How about him?" "How about her?" "Yo, Huey, stop the car!"

They want to hit up a woman they see in a driveway, but I'm thinking about those plates.

"Let's go up the street a little," I say.

"Man, stop the fucking car."

"Just a little further."

Finally I park up the street. Ro puts the stocking on his face, leaps out with the gun, and runs up on this woman. She has to be about thirty-five. She's getting out of her car, bags in hand, probably has just been to the mall. Pink fleece, lycra pants, highlighted hair, the full-on suburban mom uniform. I can't tell, but I think I see a car seat with a kid in it too, which makes my heart sink.

Ro's a strapping guy, well over six feet, with a stocking-mask on. He runs up on her and puts the gun right to her head.

"Give it up!" he shouts.

The next part of the story is the part I can't believe. The white woman sees the gun but doesn't scream. She just looks back at him and shouts—I mean *shouts*:

"No FUCKING way!"

Holy shit, I think. Who is this, the Pink Power Ranger?

Ro, a little surprised, pulls the gun away and cocks that thing back, puts it back at her head.

"You hear what the fuck I said? Try me if you want."

The minute I see that, my heart starts racing two hundred beats a minute. I'm terrified. I've fired that gun a few times, so I know how sensitive it is and how powerful. I also know what hollow tips are designed to do. And that thing has a hair trigger. I'm talking, a strong gust of wind will make it go off.

Worse, Ro has the least sense among us, and the least to lose. He probably already has bodies on him. My mind is flying in different directions.

"Give me the fucking money!" he shouts again.

Mom hesitates again. She's staring back at him with eyes like saucers. What's she thinking? What she'll tell her friends at the PTA? I can't imagine.

"Bitch," Ro says slowly now, "I'm giving you one last chance . . ."

She stays frozen. I close my eyes.

I never actually see her give the money up, but she apparently does. I can hear the others in the car whistling with relief.

By the time I open my eyes, Ro's hustling back to the car, money in hand.

He dives in back.

"Go, go, go, get the fuck out!" he shouts.

"Gimme the gun!" I shout, tearing out.

"What?" he shouts.

"Give me the fucking gun!"

"It's still cocked."

"Then be careful!"

The lady has clearly called the cops quick because as we turn onto Route 22, I can already see the cruisers zooming down the other side of the divided highway, right toward us.

I see them coming, then look up in the rearview mirror and over at Curtis and realize the other guys still have their masks on! We're driving away from an armed robbery in masks in the middle of a white New Jersey suburb, four heads deep. What fools, I think.

I lose it. I start shouting: "Dog, take that shit off, throw it out!"

But everyone's screaming and shouting at each other and not listening. The cop cars come and, amazingly, drive right past the only car on the road, which happens to contain a Black driver and three guys in masks.

"Yo!" I scream. "Take your fucking masks off! Y'all look like an indictment on four wheels!"

Finally the others rip off their masks and start throwing them out the car windows. I'm driving the speed limit. Rule: *Never trade minutes for years.* You think you want to hurry sometimes, but hurrying is what will get you caught, so lose that minute if you have to.

By then I've pulled off on a side street and I'm driving past a golf course. Both lanes of the road are empty, and I'm looking for a place to toss the gun.

Up ahead, I see there's a bridge with a little river that leads to a water hazard. Perfect. I extend my arm out of the driver's side window, gun in hand, wondering if I can throw it far enough to get into the water, or if the thing will just go off on its own.

The hammer's still cocked and I remember thinking about the breeze from the drive, if it will make the weapon fire.

But for some reason I can't let go of the gun. I'm just driving, holding it out the window.

I'm thinking of my father now. It's not just my father's car. It's his gun too, registered in his name. I took it from him.

I have to throw it away, but I can't.

*

My father was and is a working man. Had his own Century 21 storefront and everything. He had a tough upbringing, coming up out of East St. Louis. When he was six, his own father got his brains blown out, being a street guy. So my old man grew up tough, proud, and strict, determined to show everyone that he could make it straight.

My mom is a straight arrow too. She worked in a bank. Actually, that's how she and my father met. They were both working in a bank once upon a time, when the place got robbed. My mother was taken as a hostage. When the siege ended my father nursed my mother back to health.

But my father had a little wanderlust in him. He moved from banks to computers to real estate. My mother stayed behind banking windows her whole life, counting other people's money.

We were Black middle class, like out of a sitcom. Only the story was a little off in our case. We started living in Missouri, then moved to Newark, where we lived in Ivy Hill at first. It's a bit of a rough place—has a bad reputation, anyway—but I was comfortable in that environment.

But then my parents split and my father remarried, moving to Short Hills, a mostly white town full of rich kids with Wall Street parents. My father, I shit you not, started wearing cardigan sweaters when we moved to the little brick house with the driveway and the faux-colonial lamppost.

The route back and forth between my father's house and my mother's was six miles and change, but it was two completely different worlds.

In Short Hills my peers were rich kids, mostly but not all white. Their parents just gave them cars. I had three friends I hung out with in particular and it was crazy what they had. My best friend Mike got an Expedition for his first car. Chuck got a Lexus ES 300 for his sixteenth birthday.

Then there was Courtney. She was a rich Black girl who lived in Short Hills. Her mother was on the board of a big bank in the city and she wanted everybody to know it. She was a little nerdy in high school, a teacher's pet type, but man was she beautiful.

She looked a little like Gabrielle Union, even had a little of that *Deliver Us from Eva* attitude. She was always correcting people in class and shit, which made me laugh.

In our first years in high school, when she thought I was just the son of a real estate agent, we were just friends. Then we became best friends. Later on, it turned into more than that. But that's a for-later story.

At first, she was only one of many friends I had in Short Hills who had parents that gave her shit. When Courtney turned sixteen, she got a cherry-red BMW M3.

I didn't get a car for my birthday.

But everybody else thought I was rich too, even though in reality my father didn't give me a damn thing, not even real spending money. Thought it was good for my character. We lived in a big house, but aside from that I had nothing. I had to hustle just to keep up with these kids who had things.

It started with cards. Even in a rich town we had public school teachers that didn't give a fuck. I would sit in the middle of Spanish class and keep all the degenerate kids in the back tied up playing blackjack while Mrs. Owens "taught" Spanish. No hiding it, right in the middle of class.

Every day it went down like that.

Rule: *Align incentives with potential antagonists*. For Mrs. Owens, I misbehaved, but also served as an effective solution for her disruptive students.

Always try to learn larger lessons from the dynamics of any situation. Back off and think about it. I started doing that when I was very young.

I was hustling. What I would do is I would take the red cards and the blue cards—you know, those standard card decks with the red backs and the blue backs with the angels—and if it was a face card, I'd color in the face red. Or if it was an ace, I'd color in one leg red. These grunged-out white kids I went to school with, they had no clue. So I had a ridiculous advantage.

Which is another rule: *Minimize your risk*. This is America, after all. Any edge is a legitimate one.

I wasn't even in ninth grade, and I was making money. I remember I bought my first piece of jewelry with the card proceeds, a necklace with a gold weed leaf.

I did this for a while. But the big move came for me when I was listening to music. I was a big Eminem fan. I was listening to that song, "My Fault," with the line about giving a girl mushrooms. And I got curious. So I started researching on the internet, and researching, researching, researching, and I stumbled across a site that was selling the stuff.

They were out of Europe, an outfit called Ost-Pilz.com. *Pilz* is German for "mushroom," but the site was Swiss. It was run by a guy named Ron Hartt, whose wife was a Montenegrin model. She was about six-three, while he was a little guy. It would be years before I met them. Later I found out he was the pastor of some kind of psychedelic church.

It was amazing what you could do by mail back then. I wired him a hundred bucks (thank you, Western Union!) and he sent me back an ounce of dried *cubensis* mushrooms.

And here's the crazy thing. My friends back home in Ivy Hill, they all just smoked weed. But the friends I had in Short Hills, these rich white kids, they were doing fucking *drugs*, man. Like everything. We're talking kids that had been in and out of rehab before they hit the tenth grade.

They all had that dirty-ass stringy hair and the black combat boots and if you held out anything in your hand that they thought might get them fucked up, they'd pay you for it and eat it on the spot.

One night, we were at this place called Kenny's Wings and Beer, a place that's still there. At the time, that was the only place to eat in this little subdivision. All the degenerate kids would go behind the building to hang out under the balcony, smoke weed, and do drugs.

We went back there and ate some of my mushrooms.

I didn't know what to expect, but it was a lot different from what I imagined. The mile and a half walking home was like wading through water. It was raining, and the longest walk of my life. I don't even know how I got home.

But I do remember that the next morning, a kid who'd been with us the night before named Steve Tomlinson called me up. Really smart kid, an incredible mind for math and computers. He ended up graduating before everyone else, which was an achievement because he was in and out of rehab the whole time we were in school.

He said to me that morning: "How much for an eighth of those caps? They were fucking *gnarly*, bro."

I'd never thought about selling drugs before. I didn't even know what to charge. I did a few calculations, but I was still in the dark. So I ended up asking Steve how much to charge.

That would be the last time I would ask a customer anything.

"Ten bucks a gram," he said.

An ounce was about twenty-nine grams total, so the price worked out to about $35 an eighth. I sold my first two ounces that day.

The profit margin was enough. Buying at a $100 an ounce and selling at $35 an eighth was a profit of $180 per ounce. I would later make it a rule: *In every deal, at least double your money.*

I shoot for the hugest possible profit margins. A drug dealer who isn't greedy is in the wrong fucking business. Again—this is America. No ceilings on profit in this game.

But floors? Hell yes. At least double your money, or don't bother. Keeps you from wasting time on nonsense.

After that first transaction I sat down, took out a sheet of paper, and wrote out what my expenses and liabilities might be if I actually started up an ongoing operation selling these mushrooms.

I looked at the calculations and saw the math worked. Then I realized what I was looking at, and burned the paper in an ashtray. It became a rule: *Never write down anything you wouldn't want printed on the cover of the* New York Times.

Around me at that time, the world was changing in a revolutionary way. Everyone was online. Kids were getting cell phones, taking pictures of everything, going online, chatting, telling the world—forever—what they did, where, and when.

But even back then, I kept a light online presence. I don't really take pictures. A big rule: *Keep your face off the internet.*

Additionally: *No Facebook.* Stay the fuck away from Facebook. Even if you're not dealing drugs.

In high school I was intensely interested in making money. At first, it was just a way of keeping up with all of my friends in Short Hills. They were going out to Ruth's Chris for dinner on weekends, hiring limos for dances, going to beach houses in summer, that sort of thing.

I wanted to keep up, but I wasn't getting the money from my parents the way the other kids were. I needed to make it on my own.

I decided to go for it. Soon I had a booming business going.

I quickly realized that the major areas of exposure involved the mailing addresses and the physical act of selling the individual grams or ounces. So as quickly as I could, I a) developed a network of other people's addresses to use, and b) moved up to selling pounds instead of smaller quantities.

I'd pay some kid a big price—$100 a pound—to let me use his address to have the mushrooms mailed to. One of my people actually bought himself a car on the money he made just being my mailbox. It was more money than most high school kids would see in years otherwise.

I started selling pounds to different kids in different schools in the area. Rule: *Deal with as few people as possible.* Wholesale. I was selling pounds for about $3,000, which was around $2,000 in profit. Doubling my money. Just enough.

If I'd wanted, I could have made something like $4,500 from each pound, but I'd probably have to sell it grams at a time.

My thing was, never look like a dealer. Never be that guy. Even in the public schools I went to in my life, where it was at least a little mixed, everyone knew who the dealers were.

They were Black kids who wore very particular clothes. Gold chains and Iceberg brand shirts and sweaters, with Tweety Bird or the Tasmanian Devil on them. Drove Lexuses and looked way older than everyone else. Anyone looking for the drug dealers in those schools would have been able to root them out quick.

But in my own school, only a handful of white kids knew I was selling anything. Everyone else thought I was just a rich kid, like my friends. And not just a normal kid, but accomplished. I was class president, the track team captain. And nobody messed with me because they knew I hung out with hardheads on the weekends.

This became my specialty. I could move so freely between white and Black worlds, between places like Ivy Hill and Short Hills.

16

But it was a problem too.

In Ivy Hill I gave my old friends pounds of mushrooms on credit, but they would fuck up packs. Every time. Mushrooms just don't sell in places like Ivy Hill. I'd try to put friends on, but they couldn't pay the cost.

Which meant trouble. They couldn't make the money themselves, but they also knew that I *could.* So they started thinking, "We may not know where you keep it. But we know you have it. Pay up or we'll take it."

These guys I grew up with were poor. Like, for-real poor. And they started asking for money, all the time, and I got tired of giving it to them.

It got to the point where I started paying them for security, just to get them off my back. I'd have them show up in Short Hills from time to time to throw a scare into people there. One of the best at that was Ro. Initially, I liked keeping him around just for that reason. He scared people. Big, buff guy with locks, a real Brolic, wild-eyed with muscles out to here.

But one night I brought him out to Short Hills to a party at a friend's house, and gave him an eighth of mushrooms. The dumbass chased the mushrooms with vodka. Never mix mushrooms and booze.

Next thing you know, he's ripping his clothes off in the middle of the house, tearing things off the walls of the house belonging to these friends of mine. I was standing outside talking to some people when I saw some football players carrying his naked ass out the front door, throwing him to the ground.

The fact that these kids were able to lay hands on Ro and live to tell about it speaks volumes about his physical and mental state at that moment.

To make things right, I started peeling off hundred dollar bills and throwing them at the kid whose house this was. I was like, "Get that wall fixed, come back if it's a problem." These were my customers!

That was the last time I brought anyone from Ivy Hill to my other world.

It was about two weeks after that that Ro came to me with the idea to do the robbery. I was stuck now. I said yes. And next thing I knew I was driving in the suburbs, holding a loaded gun out the window of a moving car.

*

I'm driving down that side road, clutching my father's gun. I think about what he'd think if he could see me. Then I think about what will happen if we get pulled over with this gun. A gun is an automatic multiplier in any criminal case. We'll all go away, to jail, for a long time.

I stop, peer over the bridge rails, and see water that's standing and brackish and looks deep enough. I hurl the gun in the drink and speed off.

"Yo, man, what the fuck?" I hear Ro shouting from the back seat. "What if they find that?"

"I wiped it down."

"You sure?"

"Dog, chill!"

Actually I'm not sure. It occurs to me as I sit in the car that not only is that gun registered in my father's name, but I didn't wipe down the bullets, which I'd loaded myself.

Throwing it away is the right move, though. Nobody fired that gun in the robbery. They can't actually connect the gun to the crime, or so I think, anyway. I prefer the risk of them finding the hammer in the river to the risk of getting pulled over holding it.

We're many miles away from the scene already. I drive on, sweating bullets. The ride back to drop them off feels interminable.

Right there in the car I make a new rule for myself: *No guns.* Later on, I'll amend the rule. Today it's, *No guns, but keep shooters.*

In this business, you never touch a gun if you don't have to. Never have one around, never show one to a girlfriend, never take one to a range or to the woods to fire off a few rounds. It's too much power. It'll lead you to use it somehow. You'll show off, try to intimidate someone, or settle a score. Guns create problems.

On the other hand, you have to have people around you who have them. Ain't no courtrooms in this business. You got a problem with someone, there's no filing a lawsuit. You need people who can handle themselves, or else you'll be up proverbial shit creek, and fast.

After that incident, I found myself in a different kind of jam. I started to hear rumblings about people from back home who wanted to rob me. Specifically it got back to me that Ro and his friends wanted to take me off.

These were guys who had eaten off me for a while, who were now shut out. They knew I was getting money. And they started to talk all over the projects about how I thought I was too good for them now, how they were going to do me.

Word of this got back to me quick. I always made sure to keep an ear to the street in both places. As in, "Yo, these guys are thinking about robbing you."

And sure enough, one day a band of five dudes—Ro and four other guys—pulled up to my fucking school in Short Hills. They were looking for me on the field at track practice, of all things. Again, I was captain of the team. It wasn't the most captainly moment of my career, that's for sure.

But—*minimize your risk*. Which in this case meant, run.

I took off and people at the school had to call the cops. These goons from the hood wanted me so bad, they ran up on the coach, Mr. Greenberg. He taught math, but also coached track.

They were like, "Fuck you, mister, we'll whoop your ass too. Where's Huey at?"

You can imagine how that went over, five out-of-town Black kids running up on a teacher in a place like Short Hills.

Not sure how I squirmed out of that one. I think I told my teachers it was just a misunderstanding with some old friends from Newark. Even then I was a good talker.

That's one of the first things I learned: if a Black man can put a sentence together, it throws everybody off. Teachers, cops, business partners, everyone. They don't expect it, which is their problem.

I never touched a gun on the job again. But moving back and forth between different universes became my niche. It was my value-add, from when I was selling pounds as a kid, to now, when I'm selling tons.

Stay behind the white guy.

I always had white partners.

Over the years I learned that police rarely suspect a white guy. People give white men in particular opportunities that are unavailable to people like me through other means.

So my career just evolved that way. Whether it was a partner in Bern, Switzerland, who grew mushrooms or a kid from the University of Maryland who became my connect in college, I always had a white guy involved in the operation.

It wasn't hard to notice that I had friends in the projects dealing in relatively small amounts, but ending up in jail the minute they started talking on cell phones.

But white kids I went to school with who dealt weed or worse could talk on the phone all day. It never even occurred to them to worry. Two different planets.

So I made a rule: *Always stay behind the white guy.*

December 2015. I'm on a gorgeous farm surrounded by cool redwood trees up in Humboldt County, California. This is a legal pot operation run by my latest partner, a young Stanford grad named Josh Triplett.

Josh is the vision man, the activist, who charms everyone with his positivity and idealism. He's a scientist by training who double-majored at Berkeley in Biomed and Botany. He's a charismatic, long-haired guy with a big personality, the kind of person who reflexively starts talking up the prettiest girl the instant he enters any room. The world just gives things to guys like this.

Josh knows everything there is to know about organic growing and believes in the medicinal aspects with the conviction of a religious person. He's a big deal in the California weed scene.

The farm is one of the biggest in Humboldt County. It's a family farm, actually owned by his girlfriend, Sally. She's a local, simple, pretty, and totally dedicated to Josh. He talks science and politics and she just stares at him in awe. Sometimes I feel sorry for her. But she can handle herself too.

You ever read those stories about thieves driving to marijuana farms, raiding the place, and the poor farmer ends up chopped to pieces or shot? That almost happened to Sally.

A few years back, when Josh left her alone in winter to go on a meditation retreat in Sri Lanka, three jack boys tried to break into the barn.

Sally, all 105 pounds of her, chased them off in the middle of the night, in bare feet and a bathrobe. With an *axe*.

We changed the name of the farm after that. Used to be called Happy Valley, now it's Sally Valley.

Now it's winter of 2015 and the three of us have a problem. We're planted around the picnic-style table we use to feed the staff during the summer months. Josh had another solo vacation planned, but Sally's called him back home.

"Sally," Josh asks, "what's going on?"

Sally nods in my direction.

"Huey, tell him what you told me."

So I tell the story.

*

We're not just farmers. We're also distributors. We started making so much money a few years ago that we began buying from other growers in the area, to make selling runs to the dispensaries in cities up and down the coast. We crop out over a ton a year, and we also buy from these little farms that crop out fifty pounds, a hundred pounds.

The goal is to be fully vertically integrated, as soon as possible. It's the only way we can compete with what we all know is coming—the big assault on the market by Wall Street and corporate agribusiness. Anyone in the legal weed business who doesn't have the backing of a Frankenfood transnational or a Too Big to Fail bank is probably on borrowed time. We know: if we don't own every link in the distribution chain, we'll be pushed out, and soon.

The banks started buying up farms years ago. We know a big price-dumping campaign is coming. So it's a race: make as much money as possible, while we still can, to grab as much market as we can, in preparation for the coming trade war.

That means gobbling up any deals that present themselves. A few weeks before, I'd bought twenty pounds from a neighboring farm called THCare, run by a nice young lady named Ella, trying to make it on her own.

But when I went to sell the stuff in Oakland, the dispensary gave it back. It tested dirty, they said.

They'd outsourced to Cal-Test, the largest accredited cannabis testing lab in the state. Ella's crop failed because of a banned microbe found in the nuggs. The perils of regulated capitalism!

As I tell this story, I can see Josh freaking out. We use exactly the same growing methods Ella uses. Everybody around here uses the same methods. Because they're Josh's methods. He sold everybody in the area on them.

We're organic. We use organic compost and compost teas that are purposefully populated with microbes, as a way of fighting other potentially crop-ruining contaminants like tarsonemid mites.

"What came back?" Josh asks. "What are they saying?"

"*Pseudomonas*," I say. "The whole load's infected."

At the sound of the word *pseudomonas*, the color completely leaves Josh's face. I know right then we're fucked.

But Sally turns and looks at him with big eyes. She still believes in her man.

"Josh, do we use that?"

"Yes," he says. "It's called *Pseudomonas fluorescens*, to be exact. But it's a harmless strain."

"So we should be okay, right?" she says.

He says nothing and looks down. She cranes her neck down to get below his line of sight, to look up at him. Then she repeats:

"Right, Josh?"

Silence.

"It's possible the test can't tell the difference," says Josh finally, scratching his head. "I don't know. Dammit! I don't know."

Sally goes quiet. I'm somewhere between laughing and screaming, but I say nothing. Josh recovers himself, acting like it's all going to be fine.

"You talk to Ella yet?" he manages to ask me.

"No," I say.

Josh drums his fingers. He's got long, wavy dark hair, black Wolverine boots, a full set of not-dirty-yet Carhartt farm clothes, work jacket and pants both, all the "frontier brown" color I think—that crunched-out, half-mountain man, half-hipster look that's the standard costume of the modern pot CEO.

I see him glance in the direction of the front door. You walk out that door, it leads to our warehouse, where we've got 2,100 pounds of high-grade weed. If we don't sell it all, we're in trouble.

A lot of the people who work our land come down from Alaska, working on credit, waiting to get paid when we crop out. When the money comes they either head home or jet around the world on hippie holidays, to spend the cold months in places like Bali or India.

That's where we're at in the cycle. We've harvested, we've got workers waiting and checks to cut, but the lab hasn't cleared us.

Josh looks again in the direction of the warehouse. He's still in denial. He's so used to the world bending his way, he hasn't wrapped his head around the bad news.

"I can fix this," he says, looking at no one in particular.

"How?" Sally asks.

"I can fix it."

*

A week later. Josh and I are in Oakland, at night, in the back room of a lab that's hidden behind a tall chain-link fence on a darkened side street. There are five of us, in a meeting that will shape the entire American weed market at least until the next growing season.

Every pothead from Providence to Portland has a stake in what's about to go down, but they don't know it. There's about to be a pileup in the chain of supply.

Josh's plan is to play it straight. Do what businessmen in Washington or Sacramento do: lobby. He's already put in calls to all the powerful growers in the area and explained the situation, telling organic growers as gently as he can they might be fucked this year.

After this straw poll it's been decided that Josh and I, along with two of the other biggest and most influential growers in the region, will petition Cal-Test on behalf of the rest.

The first of the other two growers is Jay Mitchell, a UCLA-educated scientist who runs a Calaveras County farm called Green Thumb. Jay is mid-thirties, clean-cut, works out, and has that lumbersexual look—short dark hair, long beard, gingham shirts. Like his longtime buddy Josh, he's a botanist and a hotshot in the California Cultivators' Association.

The other grower is Laila Khoury. She's Algerian, wears backwards cotton beanie hats, takes shit from no one, is a lesbian, needs a stool to stand five feet tall, and like the others used to be a big shot in the Cultivators' Association. That was before she concluded it was a basically a white boys' club where her views weren't valued.

So she dropped out and formed her own collective, with other women distributors here in Oakland, a group called Aurora. She's still one of the most powerful growers in the state and has farms across Calaveras. She also runs a skate shop in downtown Oakland called Blaze that's like ground zero of the Californian weed scene.

She lets artists hang their work on the walls of Blaze and, yeah, you can buy weed there, but the place is also a legit business she runs with perfect entrepreneurship. No one examining the books would ever know. She turns a tidy profit on skateboards just like she does with kush.

She's the most powerful woman of color I've met in the business. Hell, she's the most powerful *person* of color I've met in the business.

There's tension between her and Josh for many reasons, but she's here with him in this late-night meeting because we've all got a common problem.

That "problem" is the old-school California weed dealer named Paul Delhomme, the head of Cal-Test. Paul's another agronomist, a wizened, weather-beaten guy who's older than us all, well past fifty. He's been through all the wars, from the days when this was all illegal.

He got out of that, though. He followed rules too.

"I just got tired of meeting shady motherfuckers in the middle of the Nevada desert with trunkfuls of weed," he once told me.

Now Paul's the one flunking all of our crops. A bureaucrat. Halfway a cop. Probably he's resentful of entitled youngsters standing on the back of the markets he built. He leans against the wall in a lab coat, staring with his arms folded.

"Well?" he says.

Laila speaks first.

"Look, Paul," she says. "We all know both *Pseudomonas* and *E. coli* are large strains of bacteria. You know there are countless harmless strains of both and they're ubiquitous enough in the natural environment. But they're even more common in the organic soils we use."

"You want me to pass *E. coli* and *Pseudomonas* now?" he deadpans.

Laila frowns, glares back.

"You and I both know your equipment sucks," she says, pointing. "You've developed testing that's sensitive enough to catch the bacterial group, but not sensitive enough to determine if it's the pathogenic variety or not. Don't think we don't know that."

He snorts.

"So my equipment's the problem. Not that you all grew tons of diseased crop. I get it."

Laila looks like she wants to smack him. Josh steps in.

"Look, Paul," he says. "I've been talking to some of the other farms. You should know this has started some talk. There are even rumors you've got a New York bank as a partner, that these results are just a way to close out the organic growers. That's half the farms in Humboldt, Mendocino, and Calaveras. People have workers to pay. We're not asking you to pass dirty loads. All we want you to do is invest in testing that's a little more sensitive."

Josh sounds convincing. He could be a senator. Probably will be, too, someday. He's that smooth.

But Delhomme pauses, tapping his foot on the ground. His lab coat suddenly really bothers me. Combined with his disrespectful tone, it makes me want to remind him how problems were resolved in his day.

"It's a little late for this year," he says finally.

"The hell it is!" says Jay.

From there, Delhomme, Jay, and Josh start yelling back and forth at each other. I don't understand a word of it. It's all fucking scientist talk.

A half hour later they've all calmed down, but it's a false calm. Laila is fuming, but Josh and Jay are at least pretending to be back on friendly ground with Mr. Cal-Test.

We go outside. Jay, Josh, Laila, and I stand huddled in the parking lot, in the dark, behind the chain-link gates of the yard.

"Look, I'm not going to pretend I understood all of that," I say. "But if I heard correctly, Paul basically just told us to go suck a dick."

"Basically," nods Laila.

"Well, no, not exactly," says Jay. "He said he'd look into it."

"Oh come on, Jay," says Laila. "He was stringing us along."

Everybody looks at Josh. He hangs his head.

"She's right. He's not going to look into it," says Josh, sighing. "He's not doing anything."

Laila now turns to Josh. "You fucked me!" she shouts.

"*I* fucked you?" Josh says.

"You're not going to sit here and tell me you didn't spend all last year preaching to me about organic growing? You're the one who told me to use these microbes. And now look!"

"I know," he says. "I *know*. I'm sorry."

"Sorry don't pay the bills," she says. "I can't eat your weak-ass *sorry*. I've got twice the problems you two have. You have loads you can't sell. I've got two useless tons *and* I've got a store that still needs a year's worth of product. I count on being able to fill my shop with my own harvest. This completely kills my price point."

"We'll figure something out."

"What are *we* gonna figure out, Josh? Half the permitted farms in Cali can't bring to market."

Josh now turns and looks at me. The rest follow suit.

No surprise. I knew from the start how this would go.

I never bought the lobbying idea, not really. Why would one of the top lab owners in the state let a bunch of growers walk in and tell him his equipment is shit? I knew it would turn into an opportunity for me.

I'm standing next to three people who collectively are sitting on about four tons of marijuana they can't sell. They can't burn it. It's gotta go somewhere.

That's what I'm here for.

*

When I first met Josh I was just buying pounds from him like any other dealer, reselling them here and there. He sold me the high price. The hood price. The N-word price.

By the way: I don't say the N-word, and I don't say it on purpose. I don't let anyone say it around me, either. That's a rule. It even got in the way of business once.

I once had a connect in California, a big grower named Sly. He was a wizard with a warehouse. He used to take me on vacations to Tahoe. On one of those trips, he was driving, blasting Young Dolph on the stereo, rapping along, saying N-word this, N-word that.

And I said to him, "Dog, you're not going to do that with me in the car."

He said what white people always say: "No, it's cool, that's just how I was raised. My homeboys back home think it's okay."

"Well," I said, "your homeboys aren't here now. So shut the fuck up."

He glared back at me. I was worth money and I was a real N-word, not one of his trailer park homeboys from Hayward. It was tense.

Next thing I knew, we heard a voice from the back seat. It was his girlfriend, a beautiful young woman named Daisy with copper hair who was way out of his league. But she had a thing for bad boys.

She said, "Sly, he said he doesn't like it."

That night, Sly beat the shit out of Daisy for talking that way in front of me. He was abusive that way. I didn't like that at all. To make a long story short, I ended up sleeping with his girl and taking six pounds from him.

It seemed like a good idea at the time.

In retrospect, though, it was stupid. I lost the connect. And lost a lot of money. So that became a rule: *Don't fuck with nobody else's girl, not even an enemy's.*

Anyway, there is such a thing as a hood price. There's a double-standard built into the drug game. If you're Black, they're going to soak you for more. Even I do it sometimes. Why? Because there's built-in extra cost, doing business in the hood.

See, there's less money in inner city neighborhoods, so you're always giving out pounds on credit. When you deal in credit, there's always a chance of your money not coming back. People are more inclined to run off and rob.

There's more violence and more cops. More danger means more money spent on security and more on lawyers. So it just flat-out costs more to deal to Black people.

For a while, the white people I bought from would only sell to me at the hood price. When I was buying pounds of weed for $1,250, I knew white boys who were buying the same shit for $900 or even $800.

When I first met Josh, he was selling to me at that high price. But he quickly figured out that I knew what I was doing. And started bringing me out to Sally Valley.

Which was good from my side, because I have a rule: *Know your market.*

I thought I knew what he was up to, because I'm the same way. I don't have time to bother with friendships just for the sake of friendships. There's gotta be a reason. It was probably the same with him. Even if it was unconscious, he had an ulterior motive.

The weed business is technically legal here, but it's never come completely out of the shadows. It's stayed half-legit, half-underworld.

Everyone knows the legal weed market isn't even big enough to keep the lights on in California's farms. So we have to move a lot of crop to other places, like the East Coast.

People out there grow their local bud, which is usually terrible. Like in Maryland it's called *kind bud*. In Florida you'll get something called *Kryppy* or *Kryptonite*. In New York, the strain is *sour*. Matter of fact, I bought New York *sour* in Amsterdam once, just for the hell of it.

In terms of the high, it's all crap compared to California weed. Which is why you buy ours.

But we wouldn't be selling California weed to you unless it was fucked up, unless it came from a situation like this one, a bad load. If you're smoking weed outside of California, you have no idea what you're smoking—mold, bacteria, fungi, all kinds of shit. Most Cali tree that goes out of state would never pass regulations. I never tell anyone that, though.

I became Josh's liaison between the two sides of the business. No other farm in the area had someone like me on staff. I became a resource for the whole community in Humboldt, Mendocino, and Calaveras, which in turn enhanced Josh's stature.

And now I was going to be put to work.

*

Right there in the parking lot of the lab, the other owners and I made a deal. Josh was still hesitant, but I figured he'd come around. Still, before I knew it, I was loading duffel bags into my trunk and driving my Toyota slowly out the lab's gates. My rear bumper scraped the curb as I backed out. I would have to make many more trips to each of the respective farms.

And once word got out, more calls would come.

I drove to my safe house, which is a lady friend's house in an Oakland apartment building.

Truth be told, the lady friend is Courtney, my old friend from high school. We're involved now, have been on and off for years. She's got opinions about what I do, but her lifestyle does fit with mine in an important way: she's got a doorman.

That's a rule: *Always store in a place with a doorman.*

I like a building that has a lobby with cameras, a front door with a buzzer. Eyes on all entrances and exits. You want a simple residential apartment complex, in a neighborhood full of restaurants and cafes. Not a warehouse at the edge of town. Not a movie set.

It's a simple concept. Eyes deter robberies. People are always hiding stashes in vacant homes, under stoops, in the desert somewhere. But the best place to hide anything is in a crowd.

Courtney isn't home, but I have a key. I walk in, go through the living room, and start loading bags into the walk-in closet in her bedroom. It's an upscale condo full of modern furniture, leather chairs, a high density king-size mattress in the bedroom, fine woven rugs. And the view is worth six figures by itself.

It's also a safe place. Hell, Courtney's next-door neighbor is a DEA agent. That always makes me laugh.

On the way back out to the car, I take a look in the console below the giant flat-screen TV. There's about a pound of weed stuffed in a vacuum pack in a drawer there, along with about $850 in cash semi-conspicuously lying around.

I smile. Rule: *Always leave a dummy stash.* If you know how burglars operate, it's just smart. People who do break-ins, they're amped on drugs or adrenaline. They just want to get in, grab something, and get out.

If a burglar sees a thousand dollars or a pound of weed lying around, he's gonna get big eyes, take it, and go. He'd be committing malpractice not to.

Give him that something. Like leaving cookies for Santa Claus, it's just good karma. And a small cost to get someone like that out of your hair.

Going back almost twenty years, I'd never laid my head anywhere without a dummy stash between me and the front door.

When I finished filling Courtney's closet, I sat down in her living room, pulled up Wickr on my phone, and started to make some calls.

4

Don't snitch.

My father knew early. He knew when I was in high school, I think. Made things tense between us, because I didn't respect how he handled it.

There was a different standard for me. When I was a senior in high school, my parents found a receipt for a home pregnancy test I'd bought. Courtney and I were together by then, and we'd had a scare.

Instead of confronting me directly, or having a civilized talk with me about it—hell, my parents never even gave me the birds and the bees speech—my father and his wife made a scene.

They bypassed me directly, went to Courtney's house. And my dad put his finger in the face of her father. He started shaming her in front of the whole family.

He started saying: "Your daughter's corrupting our son, and she's lying to you. She's a liar."

And they told Courtney and me: "If you have kids and have a dependent, you're both out on the fucking street."

Whatever. Courtney turned out not to be pregnant anyway. Also, we broke up shortly after, for the first of about a dozen times.

I bring this up because years later, when my younger sister got pregnant, it was all love. Now my dad and his wife were like, it's okay, honey, we'll raise the baby together. They let her move back home, they built her a nursery, and so on.

It was the opposite of what my father said the deal would have been for me.

So I'm just like, "All right, man." I mean, I'm not mad at the kid. But my attitude to my parents from that point was like, "Fuck y'all both."

What really bothered my father was that I had my own money.

The summer after my first year in college, I started talking about buying my own car.

My dad said, "I'll match whatever money you save toward it." Like he was being magnanimous.

And I said, "Seriously?"

"Yes, seriously," he said.

So I came back the next day with six grand. Put it right on the kitchen counter.

"All right, I'm ready," I said.

He said, "Where'd you get it?"

I was like, "Dad, come on now, you know."

"Where'd you get it?" he repeated.

"You know," I said, staring back.

And he said to me—just like a police officer—"Either you can show me where you got it from, or I'm not matching you."

So the next day, I came back with the exact same car he had. It was another gold Infiniti, only mine was brand new. Not the most common car, so it was obvious I was buying *his* car.

Beyond that, I pulled all the speakers out, and put bigger ones in. At that time, XM was a new feature, and I bought that too. Boss equalizers, vented subwoofers in the back, all kinds of shit. I upgraded the whole damn thing and came back and stacked the boxes in his garage for him to see.

He walked in the garage, took one look, and just shook his head.

I was like: "Dog, you said that you would help me with this, but obviously I don't need your fucking help with this."

It started to be like that. I copied stuff he did just to tweak him. My dad liked Coogi clothes, wore them all the time. But he had to work his whole life to afford them.

I wore Coogi sweaters in *high school*.

One time, I remember, I spilled some of his cologne. It was Bulgari. And I spilled it, and he made a big deal out of it. Shouted from one end of the house to the other.

The next day I came in and bought the same cologne, but it was the big size.

It was twice as big as his shit.

I would do stuff like that. Just to be like, "All right, dog."

*

My father broke his back his whole life and was proud of the little bit of something he had in the end. He believed in America, and thought that little reward he got meant America believed in him back.

I believe in money. So does America. Beyond that we don't have a relationship.

I went to an excellent historically black college, Bethune-Cookman, down in Florida. I was class president and had my choice, and that's where I wanted to go.

Even my dad was proud for a minute. But when I got down there, I realized I had a problem.

Black college students don't buy mushrooms.

For help, I turned to a white dude from Short Hills named, I kid you not, Charlie Brown. Charlie had been a weed dealer in my high school. Now he was still a weed dealer, only in College Park, at the University of Maryland.

I say: "Charlie, I'm trying to come visit you."

"Come on up," he says.

I take a train up. Once there I give him a pound of mushrooms.

He's like: "Hang on."

He goes away. When he comes back two hours later, he's got about three grand. I mean he turned over a pound in two hours. This was unheard of, and he didn't need credit. They take drugs *for real* at the University of Maryland.

Pretty soon his re-up was ten pounds every two weeks. That worked out to about $40,000 a month for me, tax-free. Not bad for a college kid. At first these were straight cash deals, but then we started to barter.

I'd give Charlie mushrooms, and he'd give me weed, which I'd sell at my school.

I started thinking about how to wash my money. At first I tried to host parties near campus. I figured I'd rent out halls in local hotels, or nightclubs, then account for the money through door tickets.

But club owners and hotels wouldn't rent to me. So I had to bring Charlie down from Maryland. When club owners saw I had a white partner, they totally changed their tune.

Inwardly I was pissed. But I focused on the money. Again, I never believed in America enough to be disillusioned anyway. Suddenly I was hosting big weekend bashes.

I stopped paying attention to my scholastic work. I-95 and Amtrak became my classroom. Soon, the stuff I was getting from Switzerland wasn't enough. I started hunting in the Florida wilds for mushrooms.

The thing is, before I sold even a single mushroom back in high school, I'd become a mushroom expert. I researched them up and down before trying one the first time.

Something clicked. I determined it was something I wanted. Like I was drawn to fucking mushrooms somehow.

For instance, if you touch the stem of a *cubensis* mushroom, put pressure in just the right place, it will bruise blue. That's a good indicator. Another, frankly, is if it's growing in shit.

I started driving across Florida, jumping fences, walking through cow pastures, picking mushrooms off cow pies.

My dorm room became a drying station. I had mushrooms laid out on newspaper over the entire floor and set up fans. When they were nice and dry, I'd ship them off to Maryland.

To increase my output I brought on a dorm-mate, an Orlando kid named Melvin who was on probation for something dumb, selling weed back home I think. He was a skinny guy, a little nervous for my tastes, but otherwise dependable.

Melvin came out with me on farm runs. He didn't like mushrooms much. He wasn't curious about the different species, didn't want to know the chemistry or biology of them. Frankly, he thought it was weird that I did. He gave me shit about it all the time.

I was always schooling him. I'd say: you have to bend over and stick your face right in the cow shit, and run your eyes all the way over the pie, from one end to the next. If the sheer force of the smell doesn't make your hair stand on end, you're not doing it right.

Once, on a run in Seminole County, he shook his head watching me work.

"Huey," he said, "this shit is repugnant."

"Hang on."

I picked a *cubensis* specimen, stood up, and held it to his face, pressing the stem. In almost a beckoning way, it flushed scarlet.

"Money," I said, bagging it.

Click!

We looked up. Standing before us was a big, hulking, red-faced Florida farmer. He was central casting: mesh hat, sunburn, and shotgun. He was aiming a 20-gauge pump-action at us. A Browning, I think. The sound we'd heard must have been the pump.

Melvin took one look and started running. I remember seeing him plop his Nikes in about six cow pies in a row as he sprinted for the fence.

I took off after him.

*

A few minutes later. We're driving back toward campus. Melvin's behind the wheel of my car, talking a mile a minute, trying to light a cigarette as he drives.

"Goddamn, Huey!" he shouts, failing to get the lighter to catch. "We almost got shot over a motherfucking mushroom!"

"Slow down," I say. "And put that shit out. This is my car."

"Nah, nah, fuck that," he says. "That man almost killed my ass. And look at my shoes, dog."

He looks down at his shoes. Involuntarily, my eyes follow his. That's when we hear the thud.

The kid whose bicycle we hit saw enough of the plate. He was in a hospital for a while. I'd forced Melvin to pull over to call an ambulance from a payphone, but it was no use telling that to the police, or to point out that I wasn't behind the wheel, especially since I wouldn't say who *was*.

When the sheriffs knocked on my door my first instinct was just to make things right and tell the truth—leaving out the drugs part, of course—but I was put off by the look of excitement in their eyes. You'd have thought they'd picked up the Gainesville Ripper. Apparently they didn't solve too many felony cases.

A county prosecutor said to me: "You wanna tell that story to an Orlando jury?"

He stood up and theatrically waved a hand to the door, as if to say, *Go ahead, the all-white jury is that-a-way.*

He was acting like he was in a movie. I was like, "Dog, there are no cameras in here, you can relax."

In truth, his excitement scared me. I made bail, then ran. I wasn't going through this process with just my court-appointed attorney. She was a well-meaning, but disheveled-looking, white woman who always looked pressed for time. I later read these people can have five hundred cases a year.

The one thing she did is get permission for me to attend my grandfather's funeral. It was my mom's father who died. That was in Alabama. Not exactly a high moment in the history of my relationship with my parents.

My father asked, as the coffin was lowered: "What are you going to do now?"

I kept my mouth shut. That night I drove to Atlanta and got on a flight to Helsinki, Finland. From there I made my way to Switzerland and hooked up in person finally with my connect, Ron Hartt. There, I started to build up a war chest, shipping mushrooms back home.

From time to time I'd talk to my mother by phone. Once, she said she'd lost twenty-five pounds from stress, because the police were calling her so often. My father said the U.S. Marshals were threatening to talk to his bosses.

So when I had enough money to be properly represented, I came home to take my medicine.

Rule: Always get a paid lawyer. And get the best one there is.

I had fifty grand, which was just enough to hire Carl Andrews, the best black lawyer in the state. He's the reason I'm not telling this story from behind bars.

I told him: "I want to be able to be a lawyer when I get out."

"I'll do the best I can," he said.

Another rule I have: *Always under-promise and over-deliver.* Carl over-delivered. I'd have to do a year, but with good behavior, the charge would disappear.

When we got discovery, I learned the main evidence against me was a statement from Melvin. They found his prints on the wheel, and he was in the system.

I was just a kid, but this is when I learned the fundamental truth of the American criminal justice system: cops can't make cases without snitches. They're always leveraging us against one another.

Today, I always give a head nod to Black people I see on the street. I judge them when or if they don't nod back. I do this

42

because Black folks are made to be fearful of each other. My thing is an act of resistance against that.

I try to learn something from every experience, but prison is designed to be an experience from which one learns nothing. The most you can accomplish is to keep your humanity from going backwards, and you have to fight hard to achieve that.

*

It was filthy inside. If you were in solitary, guys would piss into cups and throw the piss through your talk hole. They'd throw feces at you, put it in your food.

The prison was overrun with staph infections. It was a full-blown MRSA epidemic. They didn't use the scientific name. The guards just called it "growths," and cut chunks out of guys.

I survived because every time I went anywhere, I carried bleach. I took bleach into the shower, bleached the floor, bleached the shower handle, poured bleach on my slippers and feet.

I was in there during Hurricane Katrina, which was just across the Gulf, a few hundred miles away. We heard stories on the radio of Louisiana prisoners drowning in floods, water rising up above the ceilings of their cells.

The weather outside in Florida was wild, too, and the power went out. The AC got cut and it was hot as fuck. Guys were screaming all night as they watched the rain through the bars.

My cellmate at the Jefferson Davis Correctional Facility in Sanford, Florida was a wild white boy from Daytona named Jesse. They put us on a cleaning detail. Every night, Jesse and I cleaned the showers and whatever else had to be cleaned.

One night the guards said to us: "You need to clean some shit up in solitary."

We went down there, and the mess was a guy who'd killed himself. He'd taken a shaving razor and cut his neck, ear to ear.

They didn't tell us what to do, just gave us some rags and this gravelly shit that was supposed to soak up blood.

The dead man was white, someone I knew a little. Couldn't have been more than twenty. On his face was a stringy little reddish goatee. It occurred to me the beard was probably still growing, but the eyes of the boy's body were dead.

We stood there staring for a minute. Then I remember kneeling in the kid's blood and going to work. Nothing could make the place clean.

Later I noticed anyone who got put in that cell went crazy. Down the road, when I got sent to solitary there myself after a cafeteria fight, *I* went crazy.

The air was so bad in that room, I started blowing my nose first until it bled, then until it stopped clotting. I was yelling for the guards, but they didn't do a damn thing.

I bled so much that I wrote the word BLOOD in huge letters, across the wall, in my own blood.

When the guards came by, they were furious. "That's a gang sign!" they said.

I rolled my eyes and shouted: "That's not a gang sign. It's my fucking blood!"

They went away.

One thing guys do in solitary is walk up to their doors, then turn around so they're facing the other way. Then they kick their feet backwards into the door as loud as they can, whole days long.

I would sit there for hours, bleeding out of my nose, listening to that sound: *Bang! Bang! Bang!* And I'd think: no society that has an interest in maximizing its human capital would dream up a system like this. All it does is turn normal people into crazy people. Sick people.

Fuck that, I'd think.

On my last day inside, I went to the door, turned around, and banged it myself for the first time. Six straight hours I did this. When the guards finally came to shut me up, I stopped, just long enough to shit on my mattress. Then I stopped up the toilet with whatever was in the cell, screamed, pulled my hair, and waited to be taken upstairs.

They took me back to my cell. I gave away all my clothes and my commissary on the way out, saying: "I'm never coming back to this motherfucker."

I exited with what you might call a healthy disdain for police. I know what a trap-and-trace is because it was in my discovery documents. I studied a lot about the law from that experience.

Mostly I learned: police fill the prisons with everyone they can because getting brothers to snitch and throw each other in holes is all they know how to do. Actual police work, they can't or won't do. Which is how I walked out, a year later, still with no record tying me to drugs in any way.

If they'd bothered to ask a question or two, they might have found me out. But I was just another Black kid they had something on, and that was enough for them. America and I, we were two ships that passed in the night. The mindless experience of prison was the only thing we ever shared.

When I got out I went to Cincinnati, where my mother let me stay with her for a while. I got a square job and after a little while had my record expunged.

My real college career had been ruined by the experience. But I did come away with a lesson: I lost all my money. That just taught me to be more careful, and more determined.

Once I got settled, I did the first thing every good outlaw should do in this country.

I got a job.

Always have a job.
Having a job isn't just about having an excuse for the money in your pocket. It's a mindset.

A man with a job will behave a certain way. He is a citizen. Dependable. Believable. When a man with a job travels, no one asks him questions.

White people see a Black man with a job and they think, "You see? All it takes is a little initiative. They're not all bad . . ."

You've got to embrace these racial stereotypes. It's not enough to wear the costume, either. You've got to put in the hours, punch a clock, learn to put up with asshole customers, wear your best company smile.

A man who has the patience to work as a hotel bellhop or an Applebee's waiter is a man who's not going to get greedy and fuck up a package. If you can keep your cool when some car salesman screams at you because he says you brought him the wrong fajita combo, you'll handle yourself fine on a car stop.

It also helps you stay anchored in what people have to do for money without a side hustle. No matter what your profession is, it's important to know how the world looks to most people.

In my twenties, I found myself working at a Marriott in Cincinnati. I actually had Cincinnati pretty much fucking sewed up for a minute.

In Cincy, I thought I was doing good. All the service people in all the downtown hotels were selling for me. Things were picking up.

Right around that time, out of the blue, an old friend showed up at my door. It was a kid from my high school back in Short Hills, one of the guys I remembered playing blackjack with in my Spanish class.

His name was Lawrence. When he got out of high school, he tried college in Alabama for a while, but it didn't work out. So he ended up in Florida with some family.

This Lawrence, he got involved with some cousins, who I think were selling coke. I don't know, because I don't fuck with coke and I don't ask about it. But somehow or another, Lawrence showed up at my door in Ohio with $50,000 in cash.

He said: "Huey, I need to grow this."

I had some connections already. But with this kind of money, I needed to buy real weight. I couldn't do that yet. I was still just starting out. Also, Lawrence was a guy I knew mostly because he let me cheat him at blackjack day after day for years. Did I really want to go into business with him?

I decided to take the risk.

"All right," I said. "If we can find a plug, then I got the market. Between Ohio, Michigan, and Indiana, we can do whatever we want right here."

He starts calling around. It's all shady. One of his crazy cousins puts us in touch with some people in Miami who supposedly have a line on some Kryppy.

We go down there, to—where? I'm not sure exactly to this day. It was in a La Quinta somewhere, that much I remember. But it damn sure wasn't Miami Beach.

The problem with Lawrence is that he never got over his gambling problem. He'd gone straight from getting beat by me for a few bills in high school to losing thousands at blackjack in casinos. This dude would bet on paint drying.

We go down there to Miami to do this thing, and right away he is jonesing for a trip to a casino. There's one in Fort Lauderdale, it turns out, a new place that had just opened called the Seminole Hard Rock.

We go over. He's losing immediately. I don't fuck with gambling for the most part, so I'm just watching. He keeps egging me on. My mind isn't on the tables. I'm thinking that we need to swap some of our smaller bills into hundreds anyway, and this is a good place for it.

Two rules apply here: *Always keep your money neat.* And: *Patronize casinos.* Not for the gambling—just the opposite. Casinos are great for swapping denominations of cash.

I tell Lawrence: "If you give me a hundred bucks, I'll play. But bring $20,000 in fives too."

He gives me a hundred and all the fives I asked for from our stash. I toss $5,100 on the table and ask for all black chips back, with just $100 in reds. I play the red chips into nine hundred.

Pretty soon the management comes over and offers to comp us for our meal. We start running up the check—I'm talking the most expensive steak, the most expensive bourbon. We think we're real smart.

We go back to the tables and lose it all. I think I walk outta there with his $100 bill and that's it. Fortunately I didn't let him touch the rest of the fifty thousand.

But I kept that thought in my mind, that this guy, sooner or later, is going to get in a hole with money and cause a problem.

The next day we wake up, hungover, having to go to the meet. We drive over. Soon we're sitting in a cheap hotel room in some ass-end part of Miami. His cousins' friends are late.

I'm not happy. Dealing with strangers who aren't on time, while you're sitting around in a strange room with a bag full of money, is not fucking comfortable.

Finally the guys show up. They're talking Jamaican patois and carrying trash bags full of weed. I'm talking actual garbage bags, with twist ties and everything. Sad to say, the weed inside fit the bags it was transported in. It's low-grade Kryppy, dirt weed.

But what can we do? We're a store with empty shelves at the moment. So we buy some pounds and ship them back to Ohio.

Rule: *Trust the postal services.* They do a good job, those folks. Most of the big companies really are as dependable as their commercials claim.

In this case we wrap bunches of pounds into a box and ship them back to the leasing office for my apartment back in Cincy, which is actually on the first floor of the broken-down building where I live. I live on the second floor in a nowhere part of town, no place you'd ever look for a person.

We fly home. We go into the leasing office. I take one look from afar and nearly have a heart attack.

Somehow the box has opened mid-journey. But the UPS people, trying to provide good customer service, have patched the box back up best they could. You can still see this big batch of weed sticking out the box, but they delivered that shit.

So long as you pay the bill, America doesn't care sometimes.

We take the box back to my place. I open it up. It's all there. We start distributing the Florida dirt weed to my people around the city.

It's turning over, but the reviews aren't good. The quality isn't there. I lean over to Lawrence:

"This work," I say, "is not the move."

"Where can we find some fire?" he says.

I think on that. It occurs to me to call my boy Jerome. He's another person I know from back in my high school days, from Ivy Hill. Only other Black man I ever met who could sell mushrooms. He lived in Jersey then, but his family was from all over, mostly from DC and Detroit.

Rule: *Try to work with people you know.* Too many people out there snitching.

I first met him through Curtis, my football-player friend. We were about to buy some weed and he brings this guy along. He's tall, lean, and not saying much, a little like me.

I'm suspicious. I say, "Where are you from?" He says, "Detroit." I say, "Show me your driver's license."

Back then, I actually thought if a cop opened his wallet, it would have a big-ass badge inside. Like, "You got me, I'm a cop." I'm not sure what I was thinking.

Jerome opened his wallet, there was a Michigan driver's license in there, and I trusted him after that. I quickly discovered he had a real good head on his shoulders.

Later he left Jersey and ended up tending bar at the Sequoia in DC. All the big politicians and hotshots came in and out of there. I met Morning fucking Joe at the bar there once. Jerome was all smiles at work, but in between he was dealing all over the city, through all the waiters and maids and laundry people.

In DC, once you get wired into the service industry, it's on and poppin'. Jerome was walking out of work with doggie bags of cash every night.

But he eventually moved back to Detroit. He had a pretty good thing going there too. He was working out of a downtown theater. I visited him once up there and ended up smoking with some big-time rappers.

Now I've got this Lawrence situation. I call Jerome and tell him my problem.

He says: "Come on up. And bring your boy with you."

6

Keep the purse small.

Lawrence and I drive up there, with $30,000 in a Gap backpack. It quickly becomes clear that whatever Jerome had going on in DC, he's not at the same level here. He's got a few customers at the theater, but beyond that, he's taking it easy.

He doesn't have an easy way to get us what we need. We jump in the car—a big loud Detroit muscle car, a Charger I think—and he tells Lawrence to start driving. We're three kids driving around Detroit with $30,000 in cash, with Jerome just scrolling through his cell phone.

Just as we did in Miami, we have to go to a casino first to swap out for larger denominations. We have to drag Lawrence out of there when Jerome gets his first call back.

He hooks up with some white boys, who tell him to meet behind a restaurant. We get there in that loud car and Jerome and I jump out.

There are four of us, two white and two Black. We're standing in the shadows behind a restaurant, next to a dumpster, carrying bags of cash and weed.

We look like a goddamn Supreme Court case waiting to happen.

Later I'll make two rules based on this scene.

One: *If you can't afford a hotel room, I'm not doing business with you.*

People in this business are always getting in touch and wanting to meet on the side of the road, or in a salt flat.

Nuh-uh. Invest in a hotel room or bring me to your house. Otherwise, goodbye.

The other rule: *No business at night.* Nothing good comes of it. Among other things, you get antsy at night, sped up. You will make bad decisions.

Like with these white kids: they've got a couple of good pounds, but I don't want a couple of pounds. I want to unload the whole $30,000 somewhere, and I'm thinking I've got to do it tonight, because I need to be back at work at the Marriott the next day.

I should be buying the pounds from the white boys and calling it a night. But I make the wrong call.

I say to Jerome: "Never mind this. Let's keep trying."

He shrugs and keeps calling. But if you make enough calls of a certain type around the hood, word will start to travel.

Out-of-towners riding around holding thirty bands is what you might call *trending news* in certain neighborhoods. It's blood in the water. Before long, Jerome claims to get a hit.

"All right," he says. "We gotta go to this part of town."

He names an address on Joy Road. It's the most fucked-up part of Detroit. It's full of bandos. What are bandos? If you know rural Georgia, you know what I mean.

You'll go to these places that are full of houses that used to be beautiful, architect's dreams, but now they're collapsing. Maybe shutters are punched out, glass is broken, there are holes in the roof.

These are fine houses that have been passed down from generation to generation. People were once proud of these homes. But after the neighborhood's been ravaged long enough by crack and joblessness and violence, they lose their way, and finally get passed down to kids who aren't grown yet, aren't responsible.

The Joy Road address they give us looks like something hit by a cruise missile. The only structure left standing on the whole block is one three-story, lonely-looking fucking bando house that's leaning in all different directions at once. It looks like Transylvania.

My boy Lawrence takes one look and decides to stay in the car. "Y'all go ahead," he says.

Jerome and I walk up to the crumbling structure. I'm carrying the Gap backpack with the cash. It's dark, but I see somebody in the window up above, waving at us to go around back.

At least the floor up there isn't rotted, I think.

We walk around the corner to a gate. I don't like it. Rule: *Be the last person in any group that walks into any space.* It's just the way I do it.

So I try to wait to let Jerome go in. But Jerome's thinking the same thing I am. He looks at me and shakes his head.

"Nah," he says. "After you."

I'm like, "No way."

He sighs, shrugs his shoulders, and walks forward. I follow after him.

We take two steps inside the gate. The moment my foot lands on the threshold, I hear a sound:

Click!

I can feel the gun on the back of my head. I put my hands up. Voices whisper to me. I remember the phrase to this day:

"Lay it down."

You know what flashes through my head? That this is not how I want to die. I'm imagining the scene when the word gets back to my family.

When my folks hear the circumstances—shot dead in some Detroit Dracula house—they'll be like: "Sounds about right." Just imagining that scene pisses me off.

So I'm thinking, Mm-mmm, no. I'd always thought I was better than this. If I go out, I don't want it to be like some typical everyday motherfucker.

I lay down the backpack, then drop to my knees, in that *Hands Up Don't Shoot* pose. The bag is like a messenger bag that opens with one latch.

I reach over to open it for them. They say: "Nah."

I pull my hand back, then watch the hand opening it for us. They tilt the bag to look at the cash. Next thing I know, they bust out a shot.

POW!

I start running. Remember, I run track. I clear that fence in one jump. Jerome is behind me, but he catches up quick. Lawrence hears the shot and screeches up in that Charger.

We dive in and we're screaming, *Go, go, go!*

He's like, "Where is it?"

"Where's what?"

"The shit!"

"They robbed us, and I think I'm shot!" Jerome says.

He *was* shot—just grazed, but still—but Lawrence has no sympathy for him. He can't believe it. That's his money, after all.

He drives a little bit, pulls over to the side of the road, and starts beating the hell out of Jerome, right there in the car. I'm watching this beating take place and I just have no words. Right there in the car I make a new rule. When dealing with new people, *Keep the purse small.* You can always buy more later. You got to feel people out. And of course, never be desperate. I'm looking at Lawrence going crazy—I don't know it at the time, but he has a dope problem too. He needs the money for more reasons than one. You start needing money, sooner or later, you'll end up talking to a cop in a room.

He leaves Jerome bleeding in an alley. The only reason Lawrence doesn't catch a body that day is because he figures that if Jerome had set him up, those guys wouldn't have shot him.

Getting shot saved Jerome's life. It was fucked up.

Lawrence never really let that loss go.

I make a new rule that day: *A loss isn't a loss. It's a lesson.*

*

We go back to Cincinnati, defeated. I don't have money or product, so I lose some connections. Before I know it, I'm down to hustling for tips and living off my hotel salary. I take two jobs, three. It's a rough time.

I don't know how normal Americans do it, to be honest. Frankly that's probably why so many people in the service industry get into hustling. Waiters, maids, bartenders—how the hell else can they live? On what they're *paid?* Who can survive on an actual salary?

I start saving money with the idea of finding new business.

*

Courtney and I went to different colleges, but always stayed in touch. She went to the University of Pennsylvania, then University of Chicago for law.

It was at a visit to Penn one year that I told her I wanted to be more than friends. We were out at an expensive place, but she didn't have to ask how I could afford it, since she'd known since high school what I did. It bothered her then, but now, suddenly, it didn't. At least not so much.

She said to me: "I don't want to know anything. But I want to be with you."

We started seeing each other. It was complicated, because I was traveling all over. My college career had ended, I went to jail, and came out just a bellhop at a Cincinnati Marriott, not exactly a prize in her parents' eyes. After all, she was cruising through one of the best law schools in the country, headed for the big time.

I went to visit her in Chicago just before she took her bar exam. I asked what her plans were.

She said: "I want to come live with you in Cincinnati."

So she moved to Cincinnati that summer. The problem was, she'd passed the bar and made herself a lawyer by then. Got a job in a local white-shoe firm, doing employment law.

That had nothing to do with me, but she was still technically an "officer of the court." Which meant she now had to live a little bit of a double life too.

I thought it would complicate things between us. But I think she found it exciting. And at that time, she was starting to have questions about the world, the country, what her parents did for a living, what they wanted *her* to be and why, all of it.

Anyway, I didn't talk business much at home. But she could tell when things were bad. When I came back from Detroit, defeated and scared, Courtney said to me:

"Let's forget about all this. We'll go on vacation."

And I'm like, where?

She goes online and finds a cheap flight from Dayton to Bellingham, Washington. It's on a budget airline that's since gone out of business. The flight's so cheap it's almost free. We get it into our heads that we'll go up north and then drive to Canada.

So we do. We fly up, rent a car, and drive across the border to Vancouver. The Canadians never stop you on the way in. It's the Americans on the way back that are the problem. But I don't know that yet.

We stay at a Marriott, of course, on a company discount. Like I say, unexpected benefits.

It's the worst trip ever. It's raining the whole time, and I've got the flu. I can barely leave the room. I hate Marriott rooms by then too, with their "sleek furnishings" and the "most comfortable bed you'll sleep in besides your own." I know that rap by heart. I feel like puking the whole time.

On the last day of the trip Courtney manages to drag me out of bed. I insist we go to this place called the New Amsterdam Café, which is supposed to be this legendary place for trading and smoking weed.

It's Amsterdam in America, the only place on the continent you can openly smoke indoors.

Courtney and I go in and sit down. We're nuzzling coffees and I'm sneezing into a tissue the whole time. Before long this cat walks up to us, with a girlfriend. He's mixed, with long, thick, but mostly white locks. Dude stands out. He says, "Can we sit down?"

"Sure. We don't see many other Black people around here. Have a seat."

The guy sits down. Says his name is Robby. The girl's white and Canadian-born, named Bethanne. We make friends, sip coffees and teas—no booze in that place—and talk about this and that.

But I don't have time to mess around. It's my last night. So as we're leaving the café a bunch of drinks later, I say, "Yo, I'm up here trying to find weed, man. Can you find me large amounts of it?"

And he's like, "Yup, I think I can do that. That's not a problem."

"Seriously?"

"Seriously."

On the way out, in the pouring rain, I have to shout a little. I say: "If you're serious, I'll be back in a month!"

"I'm serious!"

He gives us a number. We tip out. Next morning we drive back to Bellingham. My first experience with the U.S. Border Patrol actually isn't *that* bad. American law enforcement always takes longer and gives you funnier looks, but nothing in my travel record scares them yet. After all, it's my first trip.

So we fly back to Ohio. I'm back to work at the Marriott. We save up some cash. A month passes. Soon enough, I go on another "vacation."

I fly back to Bellingham and drive to Vancouver with ten grand. I call up the kid Robby. Sure enough, he answers.

We agree to meet, of all places in the pool room of the Marriott. He shows up with two people in tow. One is this tiny Asian guy. The other is a gigantic bald white dude with a beer gut, a leather vest, and an earring. The big man is also carrying a silly toy dog, a Shih Tzu I think.

It's supposed to be a tough-guy affectation, because it quickly becomes clear the white guy is muscle for the Asian guy. The Asian's name is Kermit. He's about five feet tall and wearing True Religion jeans. I remember because this is before True Religion was a thing. He looks me up and down just once, then says:

"I hear you're looking for some units."

"I am."

"How much?"

Twenty-five grand, I say. There's a weird echo in the room. You can hear water dripping in the pool area somewhere.

Kermit looks unimpressed. He says. "Okay. You go through Robby from now on. You won't ever see me."

The big stocky white boy with the little dog sneers at me. The dog yaps.

It's weird. But, fuck it. We cut a deal, and I get a nice load. Enough to get me back on my feet at home again.

That night, I hole up in the Marriott room and vacuum-seal everything I have into small packets. Then I go to the parking garage, where there are no cameras. I rip the rental car open from the inside and spend the whole night packing it up.

This is something I'd learned from another guy I knew, who studied engineering at Wake Forest. Turns out you can pretty much rig any car full of drugs using ordinary household tools.

Rule: *Always carry an Allen wrench.*

Allen wrenches are allowed in cars. Even Black people can have them and cops don't freak out. I fucking swear by Allen wrenches.

Anyway, once the car is packed, we hop on the road and carry the load over. Later we'd learn about putting false bottoms in suitcases and just carrying loads over on buses. There are lots of ways we figured over time to do it, because having me drive quickly became a problem.

That second time, the border patrol people are like, "What are you doing here? Why'd you come all the way to Vancouver like a month ago and now you're already back again?"

I come up with a story: I have a girlfriend who's at the University of British Columbia, in a PhD program. I was just visiting her, I say.

I can see them doing the math: what would they say to a young white male in this situation? They can't be too obvious about not believing that story. Frowning, they wave me through.

I get the load back to Ohio. I turn over the package. I'm starting to make money again. I'm feeling good, getting ready for the next trip. I'm gonna buy more this time.

I call Robby. He's nowhere to be found. Or, better to say, he's elusive. I can reach him on the phone, but it's not easy. It takes five or six calls.

Finally I get him. I'm like, "Yo, I wanna come out. What's good?"

He gives me a date, but seems a little off. But that's normal. I mean, the guy does basically smoke weed all day. If he's a bit fried that doesn't set off alarm bells for me.

I go. I think everything's fine.

But when I get out there, he's hard to find again. I'm calling and calling, and he's not answering. One, two days pass. I'm getting pissed, because I'm on the clock. And I need that re-up.

Finally he answers. Right away I can tell something is wrong. He tells me to meet him in a bar, and when I get there, he's staring at the floor.

He whispers: "Yo, I fucked up a pack."

I can't believe it. "What do you mean, you fucked up a pack? *Whose?*"

Kermit's, he says.

"The dude gave me credit and I messed up the pound," he explains.

Reader, I'm going to tell you a truth now. It's true, true, true! There's just no helping some people. You can offer them the best opportunity in the world, and it's just there for them to fuck it up.

This guy Robby—think about it—knew Kermit for years. Knew him well enough to get work from him on credit. But all that time, he didn't think to ask for it. Didn't think to make it work for him, until he saw it work just a little bit for me. He might have been scared, of course, because he knew Kermit was Vietnamese mafia. Everyone knows you don't fuck around with these triads unless you know what you're doing. They're ruthless on a whole different level.

Buying from those guys in cash is one thing. But credit? Robby's a waiter or something. And at the end of the day, his little shitty job isn't going to cover what he owed.

This is a rule I don't even need to write down. And now his problem is my problem. I'm looking at him and I can't believe it. Who fucks up a pound? How, logistically, do you even do it? Did he smoke it? Lose it?

"What the hell happened?"

"I just . . . I don't know, man, I couldn't turn it over."

I say to him, "What the fuck does that have to do with me, dog? Why are you not picking up your phone? I don't even know why you took credit. The little bit of gravy I was giving you should have been good enough to *buy* a pound."

"I know. I'm sorry."

"Well," I say. "Just call him. We'll get this fixed."

"What? Huey, we can't."

"What do you mean?"

Robby starts shivering all over, those weird blond locks shaking.

"Huey, Kermit's Vietnamese mafia. They cut off your finger-tips," he says. "For real."

"Come on, man," I say. "That's a legend. Ain't nobody cutting off no fingers over a motherfucking pound."

"I swear to you, Huey, that's what happens."

"Look, I understand you're scared," I say. "But the end of the day I'm going to pay it. You're just going to be cut out. You understand?"

He swallows hard, nods. "I understand."

So we call Kermit. At first, the man doesn't want to meet me. But I insist.

It turns out Kermit's family owns a string of pho shops as legit businesses in the city. So our first stop is in an office above one of those restaurants.

It's me, Robby, and a random Vietnamese restaurant owner in a red jacket who doesn't say a word. He just sits and stares like he's babysitting, until we hear a car pull up out back.

Up the stairs comes the big goofy white guy with the earring. There's no Shih Tzu this time. He nods at us and takes us out back behind the restaurant. We get in an SUV, go down to some docks, and end up at a seaplane, of all things.

Robby gets in the back of the plane with me. At least once, I catch him looking down at his hands.

The plane takes us way the hell over toward the other side of Vancouver Island. I don't even know what Vancouver Island is at the time, and I'm just staring down at this big wilderness of green trees, as the plane engine hums and it starts to get dark.

The plane finally lands in a little bay and taxies to a dock. We get out, me, Robby, and Shih Tzu guy.

We walk into the woods about two hundred yards back. I don't see it at first, but then, out of the darkness, I'm suddenly face to face with an awesome, incredible, bunker-style house. It's like something out of a sci-fi movie.

It's concrete on the outside, covered in branches and moss and shit on top, like a giant lean-to. As you approach, you can see—through the one side that's all glass—that it's a beautiful luxury house inside, like an *Architectural Digest* spread.

We go in. Kermit is there, sitting at this long-ass mahogany table, upon which rests the most gigantic quantity of weed you can possibly imagine.

The whole place is one room, and in this one room there are just pounds and pounds and pounds and pounds and pounds and pounds and pounds and pounds and pounds and pounds of weed. It's the most weed I've ever seen in my fucking life. The smell alone almost gets me high.

The only thing breaking up the fumes is the smell of soup or stew or something boiling in the far corner of the room, in a little kitchen against the wall. An older Asian woman in a plain black jumper is cooking something. She ignores us.

I look over at Kermit, then look at Robby.

"Listen man, I don't know what the fuck he did, but we have a good business," I say. "Let me buy his debt."

"It's his debt," says Kermit. "He's got to pay it."

"I know, but there's no reason for him to break this up, so just let me do this and you and I can continue going on."

Kermit thinks for a moment, then nods.

"Okay. He still owes me, but you can buy his debt," he says.

I get it. See, when you owe the Vietnamese, you always owe them. I wasn't really buying his debt. I was, however, buying the connection.

"You gonna buy it or not?"

"I'll buy it."

"Okay."

He nods in the direction of a little duffel bag I'm carrying. The debt's just a couple grand, so I pull that out first. Then I pull out another twenty for what I'm buying.

He takes it. Then, as he's counting the money, he whispers something to Shih Tzu guy.

Robby gets a panicked look on his face. He makes like he's going to run, but Shih Tzu guy grabs him by the shoulder and walks him out a back door like a man condemned.

I'm left staring at Kermit, who's still counting.

Once Kermit finishes counting the money, he sets me up with a new package. I stuff the weed into the duffel and he walks me back down to the dock.

Shih Tzu guy is in the front of the plane with the pilot. Robby is in the back, shivering. He still has all his fingers.

We fly back to the city, where there's an SUV waiting for us with a couple other Vietnamese guys in it. They shove me and Robby in the back, and Shih Tzu guy tells Robby to cough up his address.

He does. We go there, to Robby's sad-ass little pothead apartment. Bethanne is on the couch watching TV, in a tank and panties, watching *Jeopardy!*

The Vietnamese throw her ass-first out on the street, then run through the apartment and take every last thing Robby has: his stereos, computers, TV. They even ask me to take part. I make a show of turning over a bookcase or something.

I'll never see Robby again after that night, but for years after, I do great business with Kermit. And I learn a hell of a lot about smuggling weed. I learn how to pack it, how to drive it, and where to sell it, in almost every city in America.

The skills I learned making all those runs with Kermit would be the ones I'd need years later, when it all hit the fan in California.

1

Embrace racial stereotypes.

Here's how you rig a cross-country load. It's four cars.

You want two cars in front, one car in the back, with a load in between. Same principle as in the wild. Buffalo and zebras travel in packs too. There's strength in numbers.

And here's our other advantage: we know police profile. We use it against them. That's an important rule: *Embrace racial stereotypes.*

In business, racism is your friend. If you master the nuances of it, you will prevail. Race is everything in America, especially in law enforcement.

If you're one Black guy driving from California to anywhere east, you're going to be stopped. A Black man behind the wheel looks out of place anywhere west of Chicago, really. So use that to your advantage.

The guy driving that first car in the parade, the dummy car, we want him to be a caricature. We want him wilding out. We want a fucking criminal. We want baggy pants with a hat turned sideways and tats and a record as long as his arm. We want him to be *filthy.*

The idea is for the cops to pull him over and say, "Son, what are you doing out here?"

The second car is the buffer. He's watching to make sure the cops don't profile someone else, keeping an eye out, making sure the guy behind him is safe.

You don't really need that second car. It costs more and doesn't do anything specific other than add a set of eyes. But it's an extra buffer, one more layer of confusion for authorities. Three cars is too few, five cars is too expensive. But four is perfect.

The third car is the load. He's carrying the shit in the trunk. That's a rule: *No drugs inside the passenger area of a car.* A corollary to that is, *Always drive a car with a trunk.* No SUVs. No Muranos. None of that. An ordinary boring sedan with a trunk.

The search and seizure laws dictate these rules. Cops can't say they saw a suitcase full of weed in plain view. They need a reason to open that trunk, and if you play it right, you never give that to them.

One of the reasons for that is the fourth car. He stays tight behind the load car, so police can't get directly behind him. He's getting in the way, so they can't run plates easily. He's running interference.

Rule: *Every time you enter a state, change out your cars.* Rule: *Drive rentals but make sure you've got in-state plates as often as possible.* Iowa cars in Iowa, Colorado cars in Colorado. And so on. And you don't stop except to sleep and go to the bathroom.

But the key is that first car. Your dummy car needs to be a real fuck-up. He's gotta be conspicuous. It's the others who need to keep their heads.

*

Late December 2015, Oakland, California. I've been sending loads out of state fifty pounds at a time from the different farms. Two suitcases of twenty-five pounds apiece in the trunk of every third car is standard. Caravans to different states: some to the Pacific Northwest, some to the Midwest, and some all the way east.

The first few loads were all right. Then on the third load I broke one of my rules.

In the movies, you often see mobsters working together in family businesses. But family members in real life are liabilities. You can't walk away from a family member. Not easy to have one's legs broken, either. Once family members get inside the tent, they're hard to remove.

I had a cousin named Buddy. His real name was Darnell, but people in his neighborhood started calling him Buddy after this ugly, flea-infested dog he had. I swear to god that dog had more sores than hair, more fleas than follicles. People started busting on him about that dog, naming him after it.

It caught on. At first Buddy didn't like it, then he did.

He was out of St. Louis, the son of my aunt Sonja, my father's sister. Aunt Sonja treated me like a son of her own. Whenever I was in town, she'd drop everything to make me catfish. We were tight, which is why I made a mistake and brought in her son.

Buddy was a street dealer out there, a younger guy. He thought he was a real dealer until he met me. Then he saw what real money and real product looked like.

Buddy didn't have a clue what he was doing. He didn't know how many grams there were in an ounce, how many ounces in a pound. He didn't know the difference between profit and loss.

You might think I'm kidding. Who doesn't know the difference between a profit and a fucking *loss*? But a lot of guys are like that. Buddy thought he knew how to sell weed. But I had to teach him everything, beginning with how to keep a ledger and how to tell if you're actually making money.

Then I let him in. I figured, well, he's doing it on the streets, I'll just level him up a little. Before I knew it, he'd skipped a couple rungs on the ladder. Made him overconfident. I couldn't keep eyes on him in where he lived, but he was acting like a big fish there, shouting his name to the rooftops, which is what you don't want to do.

But then all these California farmers got in this situation, and I suddenly had to unload a lot of product. I had no choice. St. Louis was a market I knew I needed.

I called my cousin.

*

Buddy shows up at the airport. He's wearing jewelry, necklaces, the whole thing, conspicuous.

I don't do that. I wear a nice polo, a nice pair of jeans, clean shoes. They don't have to be gym shoes, they can be Sperry or whatever.

That's a rule: *Dress like an off-duty Applebee's waiter.* I know what that looks like because, after all, I've worked at Applebee's. I make even shitty jobs like that work for me. Experience is my education and education is my advantage.

Also, when you get pulled over—and you'll get pulled over, because police profile—you must talk in complete sentences, like a college man, never acting like you're in a hurry. Tell the cop a story about getting home to your parents, a fiancée, kids. Be friendly. They can't handle that shit.

When Buddy showed up, I worried right away he was going to be a problem. He'd been busted for dealing a few times, and with his record and appearance, he should have been the front car.

But he didn't want to play the bait role. He thought he was too big time for that, even though he was still only twenty-four. He insisted on being in charge, in the rear car.

We were packing up the caravan and I could see Buddy smoking a joint in the front seat of his car, right out there on the streets of Oakland, before he started driving. When I looked to see where he put his stash, he'd stuck it in a little gym bag in the back seat.

"Buddy," I said. "What the fuck did I tell you about keeping shit inside the car? You want to carry weed, it's gotta be in the trunk."

He smiled, picked up the gym bag, opened the door, and slid out of the car. Then he went to the back of the vehicle—a white Chevy Cruze, my favorite road car, dullest vehicle there is—and calmly stuck his bag in the trunk, on top of our suitcases packed with tree.

"No problem," he said. "I got you."

"Try to lay off the weed while you drive," I said. "If you get pulled over, even if you toss the joint, the smell can be probable cause. And don't pull over for any reason."

"Huey, it's not my first drive."

The load car was to be driven by another friend of his, from St. Louis I think. He was practically a high school kid, someone I didn't know, by the name of Andre.

The two front cars were to be driven by my people, Alysha and Reece, from Seattle. Reece was my dummy car guy. He hadn't been arrested in ten years, but he looked the part and knew how to play the role. Bandana, jewelry, tats, the whole deal. He was half Native American, but looked all the way Black. I could see he was looking at Buddy with concern.

"We're off, H," he said to me.

"All right," I said. "Good luck."

Two days later I get a text from Reece. It's just a period. Means he wants to talk. Not good news. We have a deal where I wait by a certain payphone in downtown Oakland near midnight if need be.

I of course don't update Josh or the others on any of this. It's too early for that.

Hours later, I'm standing on Telegraph Avenue by the designated payphone.

It rings.

"Problems," Reece says.

"What?"

"That fucking cousin of yours sent his friend home," he says.

"What? Who's driving the load?"

"That's what I'm trying to tell you. He is. Your cousin, I mean. First he switched jobs with the kid, then he sent him home at the rental lot north of Denver."

"What the fuck? Why?"

"I think to save some bucks. How much were you paying the kid?"

"I don't know. A thousand bucks? He's gonna risk a load over that? Where is he?"

"He's at our same motel. But there's nothing we can do now, we're down to three cars. And I can't be driving the load, and I don't want my girl doing it either."

"Shit."

"Just gotta hope he drives right," Reece says.

"Yeah."

I hang up. There's nothing I can do at this point. The train has left the station. I've just got to hope Buddy can drive a few hundred more miles without getting pulled over.

A day later I get another text. This one's from my idiot cousin. It's the worst text there is:

911

Means he's been jacked. Or is about to be.

Later I heard part of the story from Reece. Just before Buddy sent that text, he decided to stop along I-80 in a Walmart somewhere past Cheyenne, Wyoming.

Again, you don't stop for anything during the day if you can avoid it. On a job, you drive all day and stop only at night.

But in broad daylight, Buddy stopped and bought himself a pack of Backwoods, which are smokes that look like blunts. Then he started smoking them, blasting Three 6 Mafia on the highway with a trunk full of weed.

Reece and Alysha, who'd been in the Walmart parking lot watching in fury, tried to stay ahead of him. But he kept racing forward. Finally they lost him completely, just short of Lincoln, Nebraska.

That's when I got the *911* text.

Rule: *Always have a lawyer on retainer.* I try to have someone I can call in every big state. In Nebraska, I knew one man.

I called him and started to arrange to have Buddy bailed out, when I got the bad news.

He was already out. Or, rather, he'd never been in. Two hours after the text, there was no record of his arrest anywhere in the state. He wasn't in the system at all.

I was in a panic. Had he bailed himself out? Cooperated? And if he'd cooperated, how could that have happened so fast? That would almost have to mean someone had been following him and had rushed an agreement with him on the spot, to pretend nothing had happened.

If that was the situation, I knew I'd get a friendly call or text from cousin Buddy very soon. At which point I'd have a major dilemma.

Sure enough, within hours, on my "non-business" phone, I got a call while I was at Courtney's place.

"Hello?" I said.

"Hey, Huey," Buddy said.

"What the hell?" I said. We had a no-phones rule.

"False alarm, cuz," he said, and then proceeded to dive into an unbelievable story.

I thought about not talking at all, but if he'd cooperated, he'd already given them everything anyway, including this number.

Buddy said:

"I texted you because I saw these cop cars behind me with sirens on," he said. "This was about a hundred miles after Kansas City. And I pulled over for them. I was smoking a blunt, but it was a real blunt, you understand? Tobacco. When the cop walked up on me, I showed him the box and everything.

"He asked me to get out of the car. I did. I had my hands up on the hood, and he was patting me down, asking if there was anything in the car, anything illegal. I said no."

"Huh," is all I said.

"Then I looked out of the corner of my eye and I could see he was in a Missouri State Police car, but not a regular one, a K-9 car. I could make out the ears of a big dog in the back seat. And I thought, *Uh oh*. The cop said to me: 'What about the trunk?'"

"I'm like, 'There's nothing in the trunk. G'head, check.' And he was like, 'What if I have the dogs come over and sniff?'"

This sure is a long story, I thought.

"But I handled it," Buddy went on. "I said, 'Fine, bring the dogs over.' The cop decided not to call the dogs. I bluffed him, cousin. He let me go."

"And?"

"And so I'm back home now and everything's cool."

"Okay. We'll talk later, okay?"

"I got you. You should've been there, Huey. I really held it together."

I didn't like that last part. He was overacting. A surge of fear shot through me.

"Okay," I said. "Well, let's talk later."

"Later."

I hung up, then looked out the window at Courtney's apartment. At least there were no helicopters outside.

I called Josh, just to check in. But he wasn't available. Didn't like that, either. It wasn't like him to not take my calls.

I decided to drive up to the farm myself.

*

76

Sally was there.

"Hey, Huey," she said. "What's up?"

Not much, I said. We small-talked a bit, then I finally got around to asking where Josh was at.

"You'll like this," she said. "He's out *yachting.*"

I actually did not like that. "Yachting?" I said. "Who with?"

"Some investors, that's what he told me."

"What kind of investors?"

She told me the story. Apparently the investors were from a big company in L.A. They'd flown Josh down and were going out to Catalina with him on a sixty-foot yawl. I had to look up what a "yawl" was.

I had an idea about who these people might be and I didn't like it. The nightmare scenario all of us had worried about for years went something like this: we'd all bust our ass trying to make the business legal, just in time for companies like Monsanto and Archer Daniels Midland and Cargill to swoop in and take what's ours.

Just like that, with a few checks. Let us do the work, build the market, run the night routes, flee the cops, then the moment the gavel strikes it legal, turn it all over to the next Kennedy family or, worse, some Frankenfood merchant who moves from terrorizing corn farmers to weed growers.

That powerful interests were already angling in on the market was obvious. There were lobbying efforts in Sacramento to keep convicted felons out of the cannabis business.

With some help in the community—Laila was particularly active on that score—we'd beat that back. But it was clear the politicians were chomping at the bit to squeeze out the dealers and hand the business over to big donors.

Especially for Black people, the future direction of the industry was a major question. One of the first companies to make it big in California's legal cannabis business was called Puff Inc. They tweeted out a company photo after a harvest a few years back, posing under the Golden Gate. It was forty-nine smiling young white people.

Josh always told us he'd never sell out. He swore he'd never go Wall Street. But maybe he couldn't handle the heat.

I looked at Sally closely. "Are you worried about Josh selling the business?" I said.

She was washing a dish and didn't look up.

"No," she said. "He's just taking a meeting."

I couldn't read her, which bothered me. I kneaded my forehead in frustration. I wasn't thinking straight. My spider sense was off, like I had a problem beyond the ones I could see. I needed time to go over things.

I hung out with Sally for a while, had a cup of tea, then got in my Corolla and drove back to Oakland. This time I went to my home-home, the place no one knows about.

And yeah, it's in Oakland. But good luck finding it. Oakland's not New York, but it's big enough. Not even Josh knows my address, or even my real name for that matter.

I turned off the GPS location on my phone. Buddy had never been to my house, either. I thought: I ought to be safe at my place, at least for a few days, while I sort things out.

When I pulled into my driveway near midnight, Brutus was on his porch, hanging out with random Mexicans. Some Latino guys he claimed were Bloods were always on his lawn, at all hours. It was weird. He waved.

"What's up, Huey?"

"Brutus," I said, waving. "You got a beer?"

"Come on over."

I walked over to his place. He was always drinking Town and Country beer, which comes in big oil cans and tastes terrible. But I needed a drink.

I walked past the Mexicans, into Brutus's house, and sat by his fridge. He handed me a can.

"Blood, you okay?" he said.

I looked up at him.

"Brutus, man," I said, "I'm not sure."

Pay the plug.

Canada was my big break. I made great money with Kermit for a long time.

He and I became friendly too. We couldn't have been more different—a Black guy from Jersey, a Vietnamese immigrant whose family came from someplace called Hue—but before I knew it, we were hanging out, going to clubs in Vancouver, spending money everywhere.

Kermit was actually a funny dude. His jokes, I have to say I pretty much never got them, but he could dance. He was *maybe* five feet tall. But he could really get after it on the dance floor. It was hilarious to watch, and while you were watching him, you forgot what he did for a living.

A hundred percent of the time, you do this business with people, a bond develops. The reason is obvious. You just can't talk about what you do with ordinary people. It's not just about safety. If you tell people, they start wanting stuff.

The economy in this country sucks so bad, people don't look at a drug dealer with disdain anymore. They just think of him as someone who's lucky to have a good job. Which means if you tell anyone what you're into, they'll soon enough start asking for free meals, car loans, security deposits.

That's why you end up hanging around with other people in the business. They're people who don't need or want anything from you.

The difference with Kermit was that he was mafia, and the mafia is connected. There's no worrying about hotel rooms with a cat like this. He had properties all over British Columbia. I'm talking about all these places with names like Burnaby, Surrey, everywhere.

He had houses, restaurants, clubs, everything he wanted. We'd go out together, a bunch of young, great-looking guys, everything expensive. You could tell we had it just by looking at us. The Vietnamese too, they all dressed in the finest, with eighteen-karat gold around their necks, jade pendants—it was some kind of warrior culture thing. But it was safe to be around them, because we went to Kermit's spots.

I'd walk into a club and he'd introduce me to a girl and, well, let's just say we'd be leaving together shortly after that, you understand? The whole area was like his little kingdom.

The only problem with Kermit was, he had a temper. And it came out from time to time.

We were out at a bar in Vancouver once and he got into it with a guy. They started swinging. Little Kermit knocked the guy out cold. It was impressive, but I was freaked out.

I thought: "I don't need to be picked up by police because you decided to flex on someone."

I mentioned something like this to him. He just waved me off.

"Don't worry, Huey," is all he said.

Meanwhile the money part of it was so easy, I started to expand everywhere. I started experimenting with shipments.

I had cars packed with weed loaded onto boats and sent home. Or I had movers driving really big loads—we call them "boxes"—over in panel trucks and eighteen-wheelers. The border was just crazy. Shit, I remember hopping on a prop plane with ten pounds of fucking weed in a hockey bag, jumping off in Chicago, no problem.

Nobody blinks at a hockey bag if Canada is part of the route. Not even if the guy holding it is Black.

Another time, I brought a friend named Malik up there to party with Kermit. Malik and I went back to my college days. We met because we both dated girls who pledged the same sorority at Penn. Malik dated Courtney's best friend, Nikki, who was Premed.

Malik studied engineering at Wake Forest. He was from a really rough neighborhood in Indianapolis, but it wasn't hard to see how he got a scholarship.

The guy was always taking things apart and putting them back together. Like you'd be sitting in a diner and he'd have the napkin dispenser in pieces while everyone else at the table talked. The first time he pulled that trick was the first time I saw an Allen wrench.

I thought he was weird and introverted at first, but then I started thinking, "This is a guy with skills I could use." We ended up going into business, at which point he opened up a little more. We hit it off. And for a while it was going good.

I brought him up to Canada. We spent three days in clubs with Kermit. Malik was impressed. He said: "This guy owns this city." I'd brought him up there to help me load a car, but we ended up saran-wrapping twenty pounds of weed to our bodies and getting right on a commercial plane to go home. No problem.

It was crazy. I was selling all over. In Atlanta, I was working with Courtney's cousin. In Missouri, I had Buddy. In Michigan, I started working with Jerome again. In Jersey and New York, I was working with a couple of different high school guys. In DC, I was dealing with some of Jerome's old connections from the Sequoia Bar. And in Indianapolis I had Malik, who'd gone back to his old neighborhood after graduation, and with my connections started to make real money.

Malik had a square job like me in Indy, only his was more serious and defense-related, something about lasers and the Navy. But it was an entry-level thing and he didn't see himself making VP anytime soon.

He thought his real opportunity was in his old neighborhood. He started saving his money and investing, big-time, in our operation.

He was running a grow-op in some Marion County shithole of a house he'd bought at public auction. To fill his basement, I used to bring him clones—those are baby weed plants—from Canada.

We did well for a while, but also both learned a thing or two about growing indoors, like this: if you're not smart, in the winter months you'll be the only house on the block with no snow on the roof. Even cops can see that.

I have a saying about the Midwest: *The good get out.* It's a depressing place to live year-round. You have to be willing to work hard for low wages to scrape by there.

That's why I like dealing with people from places like that: Indianapolis, Gary, Cleveland, Youngstown. They're tough and do quality work, for the most part.

For our grow-op, it took a minimum of ten weeks between harvests. When the grow wasn't on, we focused more on selling

Kermit's weed. Which was fine until I started to have problems at the border.

I was finding that it was too hard for me to be personally involved with loads going back and forth to British Columbia. Being Black and having to go through U.S. Customs every time was just too conspicuous. You can afford to get profiled on a highway. But not on a border. You have no rights on a border.

I played the "My girlfriend studies at the University of British Columbia" line for a while, but after about four trips I could see the half-life of that story fizzling out in the eyes of the guards.

Malik and I didn't have many options. So we took a risk.

Back in Cincinnati, at my job at the Marriott, there was this little Indian guy named Vihaan who worked as a bar backer.

He was the staff clown. Vihaan was always talking like he had friends, even though we knew he was really a loner. I mean a *serious* loner. This dude was twenty-seven years old and had never got no head from a woman. You live long enough on this earth, a woman will eventually give herself to you out of sympathy.

But Vihaan, man, he could fuck up fucking up, if you know what I mean. About the only thing he did was smoke weed, but that's not exactly a resume-builder.

He had family problems because he never finished college and was a bar backer with no future and didn't seem to mind it enough.

His dad was some kind of big deal in insurance who rose from nothing in the old country and now had a huge six-bedroom house in Mason. It drove him crazy that he had a son pushing thirty with no plan.

So I took a chance with him. He looked up to all the Black guys on staff, thought we were cool. We smoked weed around him, gave him a little. Then, slowly, I started to ask how he'd feel about making some extra cash on the side.

Right away, I could tell, that was the most interesting moment of his life.

He said: "Just tell me what to do!"

My plan was to drive him through Windsor. I knew there was a big Indian population on that side of the border. Plus, I guessed, not even the Americans would stop an Indian guy on suspicion of smuggling from Canada.

When I told him the plan he was all for it. I explained to him about embracing stereotypes. He'd been born in the States, but I told him he should put on the same Indian accent his immigrant parents had.

He hesitated. At first I thought he was being proud. But it turned out he just couldn't do the accent. His own family accent!

Most Black people know how to code-switch instinctively. You tailor your presentation according to the crowd. I can put on a Southern accent in a heartbeat because I got roots there. Most Black people can. We can Southern it up in a second.

But Vihaan, he actually had to work at imitating his father and mother. On our first run driving up to Canada, I caught him looking in the rearview mirror and practicing. He'd read somewhere in a book for actors that to make the *T* sound the way Bollywood stars say it, you had to put the tip of your tongue farther back along the roof of your mouth.

Like for instance: *but* was supposed to come out *BOT*.

Seeing this, I tried to arrange it so he didn't have to talk. I put him in traditional Indian dress for the first time in his life and bought an expensive purple thing called a *jacquard* at a vintage clothing store in Toronto. We hung it in the back seat of his car.

About the weed, I was just brazen. I just tossed twenty, thirty pounds in the trunk and didn't even think about it.

He went through with no problem. So we did it again, and again. And again.

We'd get to the checkpoint in Windsor, and they'd take one look at him in his getup and wave his ass right through. Meanwhile, I'd drive behind him to keep watch. More than once they tore my car apart.

Vihaan loved it and it was all I could do to get him not to talk about it. Soon enough he seemed to calm down. And he became indispensable to me.

There were times I wondered about him. I knew: if he ever so much as got asked the time of day by border control, he'd probably start bragging about being an international drug smuggler.

But his disguise seemed foolproof and the race thing was so strong, I felt I never had to worry.

Meanwhile, I was doing so well I started to get sloppy. I started taking loads from Kermit on credit.

I didn't need to, I just did. Most of the time that was okay, because I was diversifying my risk all over the country. I never put so much product in one load that I'd have had trouble covering a loss.

Except for one time.

Once, Malik asked me for an unusually big load. Way more than usual. He was getting a big head after some of those trips to Vancouver, but I don't mind a person thinking big. I think big myself. So I respect the same instinct.

But Malik wanted this huge load on credit. I didn't feel like fronting him. So I, too, ordered a huge load from Kermit, on credit.

Vihaan went on runs by himself by then. He got to Vancouver, filled his trunk practically to the brim, and drove across Canada to Windsor, where he passed right through Customs as usual.

He was a little late getting to Cincinnati. I asked him what happened, and he said he spilled a coffee all over his traditional costume, forcing him to pull over in Buffalo and buy new pants. Sure enough, he's wearing traditional Indian dress up top, but a pair of Buffalo Bills Zubaz down below. What an idiot. The story is too dumb not to believe.

Beyond that, I was pleased. I took the whole load and sent it to Indianapolis through the mail. I mean a big fucking load, an expensive one, boxes and boxes.

It never got there.

Not long after, I drove out to Indianapolis to collect. Remember, I'd invested in Malik's grow-op too, so I thought we had all that product on the ground, already flipping. I thought everything was okay. I thought it was more than okay.

Malik, of course, was no street dealer. He was a college guy. To unload his product, he'd turned to someone from the block where he'd grown up, a local kingpin named Blac. He had been doing Malik's distribution for years. I knew Blac too, and thought we were all cool.

I went down to Indianapolis and Blac picked me up at the airport, supposedly to drive me to see Malik.

On the way, just casually, I said: "Yo, when are you gonna settle up on that work I gave you?"

Blac turned to me with a funny look in his eyes, and I knew right away there was a problem. He reached over to the center console and opened it. I could see there was a little pistol in there, a Glock. I know those triggers anywhere.

He pulled it out and put it in his lap. Then he looked over at me.

"What work?" he said. "I'm waiting on that new pack. You go ahead and hit me when that touches down, though."

This is the problem with working out of town. No shooters. Even if my friend Malik wanted to help me lean on Blac for the money, he was a college guy, not a shooter. I could always go home to Cincinnati. He had to stay in "Nap."

He dropped me off at Malik's house. When I told my friend what happened, as expected, Malik didn't back me up. He just shot me a funny look, and asked why the load never arrived.

I frowned. "I don't know anything about anything yet. But let's forget that. But we're still eating off the grow-op. What about that?"

He just shrugged. I soon realized Malik and Blac had decided to steal that money from me. Maybe they thought I'd stiffed them on the load. Malik had learned the lesson: *No guns, but keep shooters.*

I had to go home to Cincinnati with nothing. Now I was in a fucked position. Somehow, I didn't have enough cash to pay Kermit back.

And this was bad. Rule number one: *Always pay the plug.* You pay the connect no matter what. Nothing else matters. If you don't have a connect, you have nothing.

There's a corollary to that rule, however. *Always pay the plug—unless you can't.* Unless it's going to break you.

Then you might be forced to take a chance.

I was scared of Kermit, no doubt. Still am. Forget the finger-tips. That motherfucker would scatter me all over Georgia Strait if he found me.

But what's he gonna do—come looking for me in the hood in Cincinnati? A Vietnamese guy? I had one real border between us, and another cultural one.

Kermit didn't know where I lived at the time. That gave me some comfort for sure. But I'm not gonna lie. I didn't go near Canada for a long time after that. Hell, I didn't go anyplace where I might so much as *see* a Vietnamese person.

I decided to make a clean break. I told Courtney: "We've gotta move."

She thought for exactly one second, then said: "Okay."

It was the right plan. The only person who didn't think so was Vihaan.

When I broke the news, he said: "What do you mean, no more runs? How am I gonna live?"

"Live off your fucking paycheck," I said.

"Are you kidding?" he said, horrified. Just like that, he went back to being a guy in his late twenties, making American wages, mooching off his parents.

He pleaded. I told him there was no unemployment insurance in this game and to fuck off. It bothered me that I had to explain it. Most people in this business don't have to be told.

I threw away all my phones and started over.

Be multisourced.

On one of my last days in Cincinnati, I got lucky.

I was at the Marriott, riding in an elevator, working out my two weeks' notice. Suddenly, a young kid of about seventeen or eighteen stepped in the lift.

He was well-dressed, with darkish skin and hair. I thought maybe he was Middle Eastern.

He had a tiny little joint in his hands. He saw that I saw it, and looked up at me with shrugging eyes. I knew he was going outside to smoke. I was intrigued.

At the bottom floor, the kid took a chance and said: "Hey, you got any more?"

Now, I knew you could get in trouble for selling weed, but I figured you couldn't get in trouble for giving it away.

I said: "If I see you around in a little bit, I'll give you whatever I have to give you."

Later on I ran into him again in an elevator. I had an ounce left over and I was getting ready to go home.

So, fuck it. I gave the kid an ounce.

He practically did a backflip, he was so grateful.

The kid was like, "Oh man, this is great. Thank you! Here, take my number and call me if you ever come to California."

He handed me a piece of paper. It read, next to a phone number:

NATAN!

I put the note in my pocket. For days I ran my fingers over that paper. A few days later, I was still holding it for some reason. I thought: I must be crazy. And desperate. This guy is still a teenager probably.

"Natan" lived in SoCal. From a cell, I gave him a call.

"Yo, what's going on down there?" I said. "I'm trying to come out and see y'all."

He was calm on the phone: "All right, cool," he said. "No problem. Come on down."

What did I have to lose?

Time for a trip.

*

I pack up a bunch of money and for the first time, I'm flying to L.A. I'm a little excited, like I always am when I see a new city.

When I get to the airport, Natan's waiting for me. He's with a tall gangly friend of his named Gamo. They're both kids. Armenian kids. *Rich* Armenian kids. They live in a place called Woodland Hills, which I knew shit about at the time.

While Natan chats me up on the way out of the terminal, Gamo runs to the garage and brings around their ride. It's a crazy-looking, souped-up, *Fast & Furious*–style, fire-engine-red, tricked-out Supra.

It looks like a stunt vehicle. They have the whole kit: a front spoiler, side and rear skirts, an aluminum rear wing, nineteen-inch rims, Yokohama tires, turbo exhaust pipes, the whole deal.

I mean, this was the Paul Walker car from the original movie, right down to the blue suede upholstery inside, with TV monitors in the front *and* back seats.

These kids have clearly never worked a day in their lives, so I figure they must have *very* generous parents. I think to myself, if nothing else, they'll be good customers someday.

I sit in the back with my gym bag full of money and say: "Nice car."

Gamo says: "Hold on."

He screeches out of LAX. That's just the start. For the next half-hour, I'm holding on for life. The kid is trying to set a world speed record with a dumb smile on his face.

We rip up and down the hills, doing one hairpin turn after another. The views are beautiful—again, I had never been in southern California—but I can't concentrate because it looks like a long way down if you miss one of those bends.

I look at the speedometer. Gamo breaks 100 in spots. He catches air at least once.

I'm thinking, these guys are trying to scare me. Why?

I'm registered at the Marriott in Woodland Hills, of course. I'm still getting the employee discount. At the end of the crazy drive they drop me off, calm as can be, in the hotel parking lot.

I step out, and I swear, I can smell burning rubber.

"See you tomorrow," is all they say. They tear ass out of the lot.

Crazy kids.

The next day, when they pick me up, I explain: I'd like to buy some weed. I've got a little money. Can they help me?

Yeah, they say, of course. You think we don't know where to get weed in this town?

Good point, I think, shrugging. Really rich kids in L.A. can probably get anything they want. A dead body, a Hellfire missile, triplets from Norway, anything. And all I want is weed.

I get in the car.

They take me for a drive. They're zooming again and suddenly I think: this is L.A. And L.A. is like Chicago: gang culture. Everyone's affiliated. Black gangs, Chinese gangs, and probably—not even probably, but for sure, I now realize—Armenian gangs.

They drive me somewhere downtown, to this place they tell me is their "cousin's house."

We go into the garage. I can see right away, their so-called cousins are all Armenian fucking gangster tweakers. There are three guys, all of them extra buff, with Oakley glasses on, square haircuts, chins moving back and forth, wired to the gills.

I can see something else. I'd done enough growing in houses to know. Remember, I was growing in a house in Indianapolis. And I can see advanced nutrients all around their "cousin's" garage. So I know they're growing here.

Here I am, all by my lonesome, with a bag of money, walking into a garage drug depot in L.A. with a bunch of Armenian gangsters.

And I'm thinking, didn't I learn anything in Detroit? What the fuck have I done, again?

Natan says to one of the buff guys: "Val, this is my friend, Huey. He's okay."

The buff guy Val comes up to me. He's in a black tank top, dark tan with muscles everywhere. He comes up, reaches around my head, and puts me in a fucking headlock, like a New York cop arresting a jaywalker!

I mean a full-on submission hold. The shit hurts! My eyes start popping out. The air is not getting to my lungs.

I *really* don't like this. I'm about a second away from saying, "Get your fucking hands off me!"

But then "Val" lets go, and playfully digs a knuckle into my hair.

He says: "Hey, bro, how you doing? Good to have you here!"

I look up.

The guy is basically on meth and friendly. That's the situation. Jesus Christ, I think.

Once we get past the intros, he leads me inside. There, on a big plastic table, they lay out some of the most beautiful fucking OG kush I've ever seen. To this day, legendary. *Legendary.* It smells like fucking peanut butter, you understand?

I'm talking big, chunky-ass nuggs. Legendary San Fernando Valley OG, the stuff of dreams. Some of the best tree I've ever seen to this day. Later on, I'll get to grow some of this weed on my own. I'm beside myself. I negotiate my deal, buy a couple of pounds, and get the fuck out of Dodge. I send the shit home to Cincinnati, and fly back to turn it over.

*

Natan's stuff helped me get back on my feet, but I was still looking for a new place to live. I couldn't stay in Cincinnati long. Courtney was doing a better job of moving on than me. She had resumes out all over the country, and was already getting calls back. Did I want to go to New York? DC? Houston?

"This was *your* idea," is all she said.

I didn't say anything back and just turned over the stuff I got from Natan. Soon I was making runs back and forth to L.A., and the money started to be good enough that I was considering just staying where I was.

On the other hand . . . well, there were a lot of other hands.

On the other hand, a Vietnamese guy who will chop me to pieces if he finds me is looking for me. *On the other hand*, my new partners look suspiciously like minors. *On the other hand*, I think those minors are sooner or later going to drive a car into a crowd of people outside a Laker game and end up in a room talking to police.

On the other hand, though, it was good business. I kept going back and forth to Woodland Hills. I went so often, I started to get friendly with the service people at the Marriott there, like I always do.

The head valet was a skinny white kid named Scooter who'd come to California from Jacksonville, Florida. I don't even think he came to California wanting to *be* a Hollywood actor, just see some maybe.

Scooter was a stoner's stoner. He was about six feet tall and a hundred and forty pounds, probably twenty of which were pimples. He lived off Cheetos and Mountain Dew and talked that north Florida twang. His brain wasn't all there, but knowing valets, he probably knew all the smokers in the area and probably had some useful connections.

One day, when he parked my rental car, I took a chance and said to him, "You wouldn't happen to know where I could find some weed?"

He leaned over and whispered: "Yeah, man! I've got a good delivery service."

I shook my head. "No, I need more than that."

He paused, almost like he was thinking.

"Well, I'll tell you one thing that's interesting," he said. "This morning, I parked a guy's car. Real mountain-man type, driving a brand-new fucking F-350 Platinum. And when I went to park it, I looked down at the drink holder in the truck. It was *full* of giant nuggs."

"So?"

"So when he went to tip me, he just gave me the whole cup. No shit, he was just like, 'Here, kid, take it.' He must have guessed I like weed somehow."

The guy must have been a genius.

"Anyway I smoked some of that shit and it blew my mind," said Scooter. "In fact, I smoked just a little part of one nugg like yesterday morning, and I'm still fucked up."

"And this guy is still in the hotel?"

"Yeah. Said he was driving cross-country. Sounds like he's military."

"Can you give me his number?"

"I can give you his room number."

*

A few minutes later. I check in, pick up a hotel phone, and call the guy.

No answer. I leave a message: "You gave a friend of mine a great tip and I'd like to meet."

I give the room number and tell him to call anytime, and I'll be there. I don't even call Natan to tell him I'm in town yet. I have a feeling.

Hours pass. Nothing. Maybe it's a waste of time. What am I thinking, spending money chasing a story a guy named Scooter told me?

Night comes. I'm sweating bullets. I'm pacing back and forth, nervous. Finally the phone rings. It's 4 a.m. Why is anyone awake that late?

"You wanna meet?" a voice says.

"Yeah—yes," I say.

"Give me a minute."

The knock comes ten minutes later.

I open the door. In walks a big, burly white dude, thick all over, bristles on his forearms, huge hands, carrying two huge sacks. The guy is sunburned, rugged. Just outdoorsy as hell.

We small-talk a little and I learn he's stationed at Fort Bragg in northern California, where he's in the Army's Fire Marshal program. But, he says, he's got a side business.

I ask him to show me. He shrugs and takes the two huge army bags he's brought with him and turns them over on my bed.

Out pours all these different varieties of weed: indoor, outdoor, sorted by colored marker with different brand names, all wrapped in a crazy Mylar material.

I buy a whole bunch of stuff off him and the quality, man, turns out to be even beyond Natan's crew. But I'd find that out later. For this night, I've still got a lot of questions.

I say: "Where does this shit come from?"

"Kid," he says, "you've got to take a trip up north."

He tells me about how northern California is just teeming with opportunities, and particularly full of both good land and people who know how to grow the shit right.

"You can't find bad weed if you try out there," he says.

As for the man himself, he's like a white version of me. He's a distributor who keeps a square job as a front. Only his gig is the military, where among other things he can learn to shoot and repair guns, and sometimes also travel for free.

He starts telling me about the army. It sounds familiar. His world is split up into officers, NCOs, and grunts. The officers, he says, are basically spineless college types who don't know dick about how to operate the hardware on their own bases. They get all the perks, but rely on NCOs to keep things running.

He's an NCO. But that's how he likes it. He makes less, but his bosses pay less attention to him.

"Hell," he says, "The officers couldn't figure out my shit if you wrote it out for them in triplicate."

I feel the same way about police. The average citizen doesn't know this, but most police don't know how to detect at all. In cities, anyway, they have even detectives spending so much of their time on street busts, the only thing they know how to do is throw people in wagons and make them turn on their friends.

Most detectives couldn't find a department store exit by themselves. Without snitches, drug enforcement would grind to a halt.

Which is why I have a rule: *Never snitch.* It's never acceptable. Not under any circumstances.

The army guy tells me his name is Corey. That first night, as we celebrate our deal over a joint, he tells me I'm wasting my time in Cincinnati. I should move out to where he is, he says.

"Go west, young man," he says, laughing through a cloud of smoke.

So I do. I go back to Cincinnati and tell Courtney.

"California, huh?"

"Yeah."

"Where? San Francisco?"

I shake my head. "Nah. Let's make it Oakland."

She knows my politics. She knows my heroes are all from out there. She's starting to lean that way too. She's never been there, but from the start, this new city feels like home for both of us.

"Oakland," she says, smiling. "Okay."

10

Have your story ready.

Courtney and I did end up moving to Oakland. But we didn't end up living together for long.

In this business, you need to be prepared to choose between the job and relationships, romantic or otherwise. It's a discipline. I hate to admit to living by a rule from *Heat,* but in this job, you do have to be prepared to walk out on anything within thirty seconds.

Rule: *Don't get attached.* The avoidance of prison is as constant and unrelenting a responsibility as children. So be faithful to that responsibility above all else.

When it comes to women, some guys are like: "I want to hit the jackpot." They see a woman from afar and their brains shut down. They see her clothes, her style, they see she's beautiful, intelligent, accomplished.

So they're willing to kiss her fucking asshole to spend time with her.

I admit, I've felt the same way about Courtney sometimes. But I also have great relationships with people when I'm not with her. In other words, I prefer to be around her. But there are some very close seconds.

We moved out to Oakland together, but quickly ended up in separate apartments. Why? Because she caught me off my game for a split second.

Somewhere along the line—years ago—I forgot how I lost my virginity.

Under torture, I couldn't tell you the truth. I honestly don't know, and I don't even remember when I *forgot*. All I know is that sometime in my late twenties (I think), it struck me that I didn't remember.

If I had to bet, I'd say the real story was that it happened at a very early stage of my life, on a family trip to Spain. I went with my dad and one of his friends from the hood who ended up in real estate, and the friend's son, a cross-eyed kid my age named Freddy.

I was probably about fifteen, and ended up at a brothel with my dad's friend and his son. Not exactly a scene from *National Lampoon's Vacation*.

And I ended up with two Spanish girls. I'm almost certain this was my first time having sex, and it was with these two women (the additional question of which one was first is another thing I can't be sure of).

That this bizarre family experience happened, I have no doubt. I just can't remember the order of things. Because this was a secret I had to keep from pretty much everyone, I started telling people a "cleaner" story, i.e., that my first time was with Courtney.

I'd known her since ninth grade and she was my first serious girlfriend. It was believable enough.

But I told that version of the story so often over the course of the next decade or so that I myself began to get confused. Thinking back, maybe my first time *was* with Courtney.

Specifically, I think it might have happened in my bedroom in my father's house at Short Hills.

I told people details about it being a hot-but-clumsy experience, maybe filled in things in my mind about what she'd been wearing, and perhaps added some ancillary details, like my father and stepmother being away for the weekend, so we had the whole house to ourselves. The narrative got pretty embellished over time.

Or: those details were what actually happened, and I just remembered them better over time. I honestly can't be sure.

Again, I couldn't say when I first realized I didn't have a handle on this. I seem to recall thinking about it over a sandwich on the road once. I just didn't think it was important at the time.

*

Many years later. Courtney and I are sitting in that swank apartment with the doorman in Oakland, which at the time we believe will be *our* home.

Things between us are strained. One thing that people have to understand about this life: it's not easy on relationships.

I talk to my friends in other professions, and they all say the same thing: travel is murder on couples.

The difference is, they can pick up the phone and call, or FaceTime even, whenever they want.

I've got to stay off the lines when I'm on the road. Especially when I'm in the middle of a move, it's pure radio silence most of the time. This creates tension in a relationship.

One of the worst things about going on the road is the fact that I sometimes have to put my hands on things, do things myself, take those risks. I've traveled across the country several times with shit in the trunk myself, like by myself.

Especially when you're trying to get back on your feet, and maybe you've lost everything and you can't pay for workers, you've got to do it yourself. And that is not a good feeling, being out there in that frame of mind.

There's the feeling that you might not get home. You have thoughts: what if I get caught out here? I'm not an anxious person, but one of the few types of anxiety I feel is this anxiety on the road. And it's not just the fear of getting caught, but fears about Courtney, too. Like if I get hit, we might not be a thing anymore.

One of the major points of contention between us, on my end anyway, is this: if something happens to me, what's your position going to be?

That's a question that always had an uncertain answer. It's one of the reasons why we've broken up many times over the years.

Worse, whenever we break up, men appear in her life. They're always the same kinds of men. They're exactly unlike me: stable, in square jobs, not on the road, not mysterious. Men who, as she's put it, look good "on paper."

I mean, I'm not trying to be *on paper* at all. It's clearly a problem area for us. And not one that can be easily resolved.

One additional detail worth mentioning:

Although Courtney and I grew up in the same place, our backgrounds are not the same. Unlike me—the son of a local real estate agent—Courtney comes from a genuinely rich family. Her parents are both high-powered bank executives. I'm not talking about little-ass branch managers, either. I'm talking about people with corner offices working for Too Big to Fail fucking megabanks in downtown Manhattan.

Courtney comes from real money, *fuck you* money. She's used to having things handed to her. And though she's well educated and good at what she does, she—this is hard for me to say—doesn't particularly like to work.

A side note: when Courtney and I have broken up over the years, I've tended to gravitate toward women who really had to grind to get it. One woman in Cincinnati I became close to had a smack dealer for a father who ended up in a wheelchair. She put herself through school, had to fight all the way.

When I asked this woman where she'd be if I got picked up, there was no question: "Get the fuck outta here, Huey, you know I'll be there. It's not even a question."

I ask this of Courtney, and it's like, "Eh." Like, noncommittal.

Anyway, Courtney does work, because the family rule is, if you can work, you work. But she doesn't *like* to work. This has had a direct impact on our life together.

A few times, she's been between jobs, and those are always the happiest times for us. She doesn't get stressed, she goes out, she gets spa treatments, she pampers herself, she's happy.

When we first moved to Oakland, she didn't have a job at first. Things were great between us. We had more fun than we'd had in a while. We went to Mexico. We had great times.

But then she got a job, as a house attorney for a tech firm in San Francisco. Everything changed. The job itself was great, a step up for her professionally. But she always came home with things to work out. Little disagreements with co-workers, office dramas, things I often don't even know about—but suddenly became my problem, nonetheless.

So we're sitting at home one night, soon after she started that job, chilling, watching Netflix. I'm in relaxation mode, happy.

But I look over and I see Courtney is looking at me. She'd mentioned before with a sigh that she'd had a bad day at work. Now I can see: she wants to start something.

Uh oh.

She starts like this:

"You know, we've been working on building trust, and something's been on my mind, and I have something I need to ask you."

"Okay."

"How did you lose your virginity?"

Just like that, out of the blue. Of all questions, she picks *that* one.

I choke. Instead of answering one way or another right away, I hedge and say, "Why?"

I'm fucked from that moment. She squints and digs deep in her mind for a comeback:

"The question," she says, "is benign."

The word *benign* lands confrontationally in my ear like a wad of llama spit. Why that word? I realize suddenly she picked that shit out intentionally, to make me angry. I try to be calm.

"What the fuck do you mean," I say slowly, "the question is *benign?*"

"Just like I said. If it's benign, why not answer it?"

So it's a cross-examination. Okay, I'll play.

"If it's benign, then why is it important?"

"You're not understanding what I mean when I say 'benign,'" she says. "If the question is benign, then you shouldn't worry about answering it."

The irony of this is that, between the two of us, I'm the one who most often has to bite his lip about her speech. Courtney has a great vocabulary, but it takes her a long time to put her sentences together.

More than once, we've had fights that go next-level when I cut her off and just synopsize what she's about to say. Her eyes in these instances always grow to the size of baseballs and she stares at me, and shouts: *"Let me finish!"*

And I say, "Fine, finish." At which point she goes on to say exactly what I said, only using more words.

Now she's telling me what *benign* means.

"I understand exactly what you mean," I said. "Which is why I say: if this is benign, then why does it matter? Let this shit ride. But it's not 'benign,' because you not only want to know, but our effort at 'building trust' depends on the answer. That's a bad-faith question, counselor."

She hates when I lawyer-talk back at her. For a split-second I feel like I have the upper hand in the conversation. But I lose it when we get around to the truth. I mean, what the fuck? We're trying to build trust, right?

So I tell her the truth.

When I tell her I can't actually remember my first time, she stares back at me like she's looking at Hitler or Pol Pot or some shit.

"What do you *mean*," she says, "you can't remember?"

"Just like I said. I can't remember."

"You're telling me it might have been *me*, but you can't remember?"

When she puts it like that, it does sound bad.

"Right," I say. "That's what I'm saying. I'm just keeping it 100. The truth was what you were looking for, right?"

"That's fucked up, Huey."

"Look," I say. "You've obviously been carrying this shit around for a long time. I wish I could tell you different. But I don't know, and the answer ain't going to change shit."

She ends up throwing me out of the apartment.

Fortunately I have the other spot already across from Brutus, had it since the first week we moved out here. I always keep a safe house. I've just never really lived there. Now, I will have to.

On the drive over, I'm steaming. It irks me that Courtney thinks I'm being sneaky. But I'm not being sneaky. I just don't know, and what woman wants to hear that her man might have lost his virginity to two Spanish prostitutes, when she thinks it was her?

I can see her point of view, but on the other hand, what does she want me to do? Lie?

As it happens, I'm due to fly out the next day to Maryland, where one of my distributors, Lawrence—crazy-ass Lawrence, the gambler who shot my boy Jerome in Detroit—has just sent an SOS.

Seems we lost a load somehow, which normally wouldn't worry me too much, except it's the second time it happened there. Two times now Lawrence has told me a shipment didn't arrive. Once can be an accident, but twice makes me think about more serious issues.

I have to find out the truth, but now I'm dealing with this Courtney mess on top of everything else.

*

The next morning. I'm packing to fly out of Oakland when I decide to call her, just to see if we can patch things up. No answer. I send a text: *Good morning!*

No answer. I shrug. Oh, well, I think, these are the breaks of the game.

An hour or so later, a text comes in:

H—You are disrespectful and dishonest and I can't have people like you in my life.

I look at the text, shrug again, and turn off my phone. So that's that, I think.

As I'm getting into the car, Brutus sees me and drags himself over from across the street.

"What's up, blood?"

"Brutus. What's good man?"

He starts talking about his case, but sees my travel bags and quickly gets to the part where he hits me up for weed. I toss him whatever I have in my armrest.

"Huey, blood, you don't understand, you're only one who cares. I'm serious, blood, no one else even gives a fuck about Brutus."

I reach out my fist to give him a dap (fist bump). Then I frown and ask:

"Brutus, has a woman ever asked you a *benign* question?"

"What the fuck does benign mean?"

I shake my head. "You know what, don't worry about it. Peace man."

"Later, blood."

Hours later. I'm at the airport, ready to go through security, when I get another text:

We need to talk.

It's from her. She's at the airport, came all the way to meet me. These are the downfalls of having attachments. In terms of business, this is a liability. I need to be focused on these missing packs. Instead, I'm dealing with this.

I sigh. I might be missing my flight now, but what to do? I go to meet her in the only place you can meet pre-security, a little bar called Heinold's First and Last Chance.

I don't even want to think about the symbolism of the restaurant or its name.

She sits down, stares at me from across the table, and takes my hand.

"Huey," she says, "I'm sorry about the text I sent this morning. I love you."

I sigh. "I love you, too, Courtney," I say. "And I'm sorry too. About the whole thing."

We embrace. I'm late and she knows it, though she doesn't know what's on my mind about Maryland. We part and I go through security, feeling better about how things are between us.

On the flight, though, I go over our conversations, and I realize she only apologized for the text, but somehow got me to apologize for everything.

Lawyers, I think, shaking my head. By the time the plane lands, I'm mad again.

*

In Baltimore, I can tell right away, something is off.

I meet Lawrence at the Amtrak station, Penn Station. I sit next to Lawrence on a waiting room bench. He's a mess. He's sweating and talking too fast. The ex-football player is still tall, but he's looking gaunt. This is the first time I catch on to the fact that he's using.

Again, I don't fuck with dope or coke. That's a rule. And I don't let my people do it either. If Lawrence is getting high, he's a liability.

Then he tells me his story, which is fucked also.

The short version is that we had a package arrive by courier that was short a couple of pounds. That makes no sense to me.

"What do you mean? You're telling me it arrived, but it's short—how much?"

"Two pounds. Well, two and a half pounds."

"Which was it, two pounds, or two and a half?"

"Two and a half."

We go over it three or four times. Something's not right. A thief would take the whole load. I can't process the logic of a load arriving just a little short.

That's someone sending a message, or—or what? I can't figure it out.

If Lawrence is using and gambling still, he could have been picked up somewhere, and this whole trip could have been a pretext just to get me talking. So I don't really say anything.

After I grill Lawrence on every single detail of this story, I tell him not to sweat it for now and turn around to fly home. The Baltimore situation is just one of many small but troubling things that have begun to happen to me since I left Cincinnati. I ponder the situation the whole way back. When I return, I don't tell Courtney I'm in town, and just go to my spot.

That's how we ended up in separate apartments. Together-not-together.

Alone, in my own spot, I began to think over my situation. I had problems, and not just in my home life. It was now obvious I had one in business too. I just didn't know where it was.

11

Travel light.

Alone in my place in Oakland, I rolled a J, sat by my window, and peered through the curtains. I could see Brutus across the street doing his jailhouse push-ups. He looked free and happy. Old, bent, and shacked up with a girl with eleven teeth maybe, but happy. For the first time, I envied the motherfucker.

Unlike him, I had troubles. Something was off in my business. I both deduced and sensed it.

I was almost done moving all of the stuff from Laila and Jay and the other Cali farms, but there was that trouble with my cousin's run that still nagged. I had two separate packs, with two totally separate people in two totally different cities, get hit. They were either getting lost entirely, or else they were arriving short, like with Lawrence in Baltimore.

Short! That part of it fucked me up. What jack boy busts open a ten pack and only takes four units? Someone actually robbing you either takes it all, or takes so little you're not supposed to notice, even if you do.

But taking *not quite half?* What the fuck is that?

At first, I was focused on Lawrence. Had to be him, I thought. He's shady enough to try it. It's always been an effort with him. Like he'd take losses, then take his time covering them. Also, and this isn't to be underestimated, he still held me partly responsible for that loss we took in the D with Jerome.

Lawrence was a big, hotheaded guy who didn't mind waving guns around and had enough size to intimidate people. He was tough and mean enough to do a little business in a place like Baltimore, but didn't have enough brains to really level up nationally.

Was that really the guy robbing me? Maybe telling me my loads were short was his way of getting repaid for the fifteen bands we'd lost in Detroit.

That plan was just dumb enough to come from Lawrence's head. But it didn't quite feel right. Something was off. And it didn't explain the missing packages in other places, my cousin going off the grid on a run, and some other problems.

I needed to lay it all out, talk things over, audit my shit from top to bottom. But how?

In this business you can never confide about certain things. If people think you're so much as considering the possibility that someone's snitching on you, now you're in danger. In a snap you'll be stuffed in a trunk and taking a ride somewhere. Like the desert. I suddenly remembered that asshole Paul Delhomme, who got out because he was "tired of meeting shady motherfuckers in the Nevada desert."

I decided right there that I didn't want to go to the Nevada desert ever, for any reason. The problem with scaling up an operation that covers each time zone and each region of the mainland United States is that you can only keep your eye on so much. I had a problem in my operation. I needed to find it. And soon.

Time for a trip. Tour the factory floor, so to speak. Look at the whole operation, see what doesn't look right, feel right, or add up. Every now and again every company needs a good audit. It was time for ours.

*

Rule: *Treat your cash like kids, don't let it stay inside all day and get soft.*

When I first started in this business, in my teens, all the money went in a shoebox. Pretty soon I ran out of shoeboxes. Living with my parents, I didn't have much space of my own, so I started getting creative. I remember I had a bunch of Belvedere Vodka bottles—I was shoving five hundred bucks worth of twenties into each Belvedere bottle, then lining those up in a closet.

A lot of dealers never grow out of that mentality. You've seen *Training Day,* where Scott Glenn has his "pension" buried under his house? There's some truth to that shit. Even the best growers aren't always sophisticated. They'll make money, wrap it, and bury it. From time to time they'll open it up so it doesn't get moldy, or even just to look at it. Then they just re-wrap it.

Up and down the coast of California, man, I guarantee you there's half a billion dollars buried there.

That's one of the reasons I try not to do business with straight-up gangsters. Because the mentality is: "All right, we know you got a couple hundred thousand buried somewhere the fuck up here, we know you got pounds and pounds stashed nearby, and we don't want to do a deal, we just want to take it."

Right now if you look at the California news the main thing is people from out of town, flying in to rob growers, do home invasions. It's a major thing, and a bunch of these guys are coming in from Georgia, for some reason. It is what it is.

That's one reason I don't keep my money buried in some moldy locker somewhere. My money is out there working. The trick is to find places to make it work. This is America, man, there's always a way to make cash reproduce.

For instance: around 2010–11, I started making money running grows in underwater houses. Call it modern-day reparations. Pre-2008, what the banks did, they rolled into minority/immigrant neighborhoods and started handing out mortgages to anyone with a pulse. Or some white man with a briefcase would knock on a door in a place like Stockton or Fresno or Richmond, Antioch or Vallejo and convince some nice old Latina or Black lady to refinance her home.

Hey, he'd say, we can lower your payment by two hundred a month. Think of what you could do with two hundred extra dollars every month?

He'd get his signature and leave. Six months later, the house is underwater, interest rates have changed, and the old lady *owes* an extra two hundred, or four hundred, or six. Next thing you know, she's getting a foreclosure notice, and she's got 120 days to get the fuck up out the house.

Laila was telling me about this one day, said she had an idea.

"Let's light 'em up," she said.

We started having people hang out in foreclosure courts and make offers. As soon as the judge gavels out the order, we'd follow that old lady, or that young janitor with kids, or that tarot card reader who makes $16,000 a year but somehow got a $200,000 mortgage, or whoever. And we make a pitch in the parking lot.

"Hey," we'd say. "I see that you're in a financial situation. I think we can help. This is what we're doing. We'd need your basement for a year. In the meantime we'll take care of whatever you owe the bank, and at the end of this year, we'll give you X amount of portions of the profits."

Everybody's happy that way. We have a place where it looks like a citizen lives here. People are coming and going, doing their normal shit. But really there's something else going on.

The people get to stay in the house, so they're happy. They get a breather from these payments, so that's another kicker. So, it's not *totally* predatory. And, as an extra incentive, we're now all partners in a criminal conspiracy, so that keeps their mouth fucking shut until the end.

If you look at the map of where the foreclosure crisis hit the worst in California, these are all areas that are very close to the Sierra Nevada foothills. So finding people who know how to grow weed isn't hard. People there are very skilled in this space.

So you find a local "tenant," you move him or her in, and you light it up, maybe one, two, three rows max.

For me, grow houses had never been a huge moneymaker, because I wasn't great at growing weed. Per light, I might make a pound or two. The people we hired, they might do better than me, but still—at the end of three, four cycles in a year, subtracting costs and the cut to the owner, you might be making $50,000, $60,000 per house, per year.

Before long, I started to think a little bigger. Fuck taking the cash out the house. Why not take the house too? After we'd done enough grows, the owner would sell to us basically for nothing, just happy to have someone taking over the payments.

You take a fucked-up house near foreclosure, and you fix it. Put a hot water heater in there, a new roof. Maybe you pull some fucked-up hardwood and put down linoleum.

Before long, we'd find a house in a decent neighborhood that needs some work, and we weren't even lighting it up. We'd just buy it and say, all right, we got cash here, let's hire some workers and let's do what the fuck needs to be done.

This made me a little nervous because it got me away from a business I knew really well. But it made money for a while. The grows were a good steady source of income too.

But there's a downside. The number one problem with grow houses is someone always tells somebody they live in a grow house. That's the one thing you cannot do, but people fucking do it.

When I was growing in my own apartment in my early years, in the Midwest, that was one of the loneliest years I had in my life, because I could have no company. Zero!

California is one thing—people are used to seeing weed growing everywhere. But you tell people in the Midwest, East Coast, and shit, everybody's friends go check it out, because it's the coolest thing poppin'. *Oh, a grow house? Really? I wanna see!* Next thing you know motherfuckers are masked up, running up in your shit.

We didn't have too much of that over the years, but there were a few close shaves. The crash years were long gone by now and I didn't have many grows left. Still, I wondered: could that be the source of my problems?

I drove down to Stockton, where I met the guy who collected all the cash from all our grows. He was a friend of a friend of Laila's, a white boy from Berkeley named *Logan Nelson.* That fucking name always made me laugh. His parents might as well have named him *white person.*

Anyway, Logan was a public school teacher, taught English I think, naturally made shit for salary and was crushed by student loans and soon after graduation found himself broke, to the point where his was one of the first distressed houses we grew in.

He was a skinny, nerdy kind of guy, who I imagined was both ignored by his students and intimidated by them. Around Laila and me he always seemed apologetic and overcome simultaneously with financial shame and white guilt. I was always tempted to freak him out by accusing him of calling me the N-word, as in, "What did you say? Motherfucker, you called me *what?*" He'd probably jump through a window.

Now I made a surprise visit, just to scratch an itch: could *Logan Nelson* be my leak? I made these pickups myself because at this point I'm not letting anyone know what I'm doing and how I'm moving. Maybe he was my problem?

It made no sense, the more I thought about it. The poor teacher didn't even know my real name (we gave him a fake one). I always met him in public places and always walked a bit to get there, to make sure the guy never even saw a license plate. He could maybe put police onto Laila—he knew her from her store—but he knew shit about me.

I met him in the Weberstown Mall, a typical California mall full of airheads buying shit they don't need with credit cards. Logan was at a Chipotle, sorrowfully eating a plateful of what the chain at the time was proudly calling "food with integrity."

He looked miserable eating guac and chips. I got a kick out of this dude: he was ashamed of everything, even the malls he ate in.

"What's up, powder?" (I called him powder as a nickname because of how white his name was.) "Enjoying your lunch?"

"I'm sorry. There's nowhere good to eat in this town."

"All good! You got that for me?"

This was a secondary reason for my visit. If I had trouble ahead, to the extent that it was possible, I didn't want to lose product and cash. Logan had a bit of both for me and used his foot to slide a duffel on the floor up against my leg.

I grabbed it, and after a cursory conversation in which I told him he wouldn't be seeing me anymore—he'd have a new contact—left. He didn't seem put out by that one way or another, and didn't ask me any questions, not like I would have answered them anyway. But he clearly wasn't probing. I couldn't see any way he was the source of my problems.

After dropping the bag off at Courtney's place—whether we were fighting or not, I had a key and her place was one of many stashes—I wanted to take a trip out to the farm. I called and told Sally I was coming. But she put Josh on the line. He wanted me to meet him in town for a drink instead, with Laila.

That didn't seem like a good sign. But we did it. The three of us met at the CommonWealth, an Oakland soccer bar, if you can imagine such a thing. It's actually where I'd met Josh for the first time. I'd put out feelers that I was looking to meet farmers in the area and someone set me up with him.

Earlier that day I'd had a fight with Courtney, and it took up the whole afternoon. The only other thing I did that day was meet Josh, and it was the best meeting I ever had. We sat down and hit it off right away. I talked to him about what I do, and he told me about his farm and said, "You're never going to need to visit another farm again."

I left that meeting on a true emotional high, at the doorstep of a new life. Now it felt like we were meeting here again to mark the end.

We got a table in the back. Josh looked harried and stripped of his usual Kennedyesque comportment. He immediately made an announcement.

"Huey, Laila," he said. "I might as well cut to the chase. I'm getting out."

Laila and I stared at each other in shock.

"What?" I said. "Why?"

He shook his head, looked down at the table, and sighed.

"I've got to tell you about this boat trip I went on," he said. "Wall Street people. One was from a New York hedge fund called Statement Partners. Two more were L.A.-based private equity guys, one from ABR, the other from Verida Capital Management. Two more were from an investment bank up in Canada called CanOutcome. They're all heavy investors in legal cannabis and they're looking to get in with the Cultivators' Association."

"Why'd they call you?" Laila asked. "Why not me?"

Josh shrugged, as if to say, *Because you're a scary Black lesbian?*

"You really need me to answer that?" he asked.

"Go on."

"Let me tell you what's in our future," he said. "They're going to pour money into PACs and lobby Sacramento till it's neck-deep in cash. Then they'll set up a licensing system so strict that the Pope would need references. They're committed to keeping out anyone with a felony and they're going to push the Colorado blueprint here, which is going to mean ten years of tax returns just to get your application through the door."

"Fuck!"

"And that's not even the worst part. They're going to buy up farms one by one and commit legal cannabis tax dollars to putting illegal dealers out of business."

"How?" Laila asked.

"By killing the price point. The good old days of $3,000 a pound, I think, are dead. They didn't actually come out and say that, but they said it in so many words. They said things like, 'For competitors, the capex is going to be very tough from an ROI standpoint.' Occasionally they would speak English, though, and my understanding is they foresee a future where wholesale pounds are gonna sell for four hundred bucks, maybe even less."

"Less!" I almost shrieked. "It fucking *costs* four hundred to crop a pound."

"Not for them it won't. Not once they scale up," he said. "Look, I'm not gonna lie, they made me an offer. A very generous offer, to essentially be a face for this thing. But they not only don't have any interest in cannabis, they have a hard time even pretending.

"I mean, we're out there way offshore, talking about billion-dollar cannabis deals, and when I rolled one they all went topside and drank Glenlivet.

"I politely said no, and that boat trip got pretty short after that. They dropped sail and motored back to L.A."

Josh shook his head. "You know, I got into this to pay for medical bills for my family. And by the time these guys are done with the business, I'll be damn near better off flipping burgers. I don't think I can do this anymore. I thought you should know."

We chatted about a few more things, then separated. Alone, driving back through the night to my spot, I found myself feeling petrified and hopeless.

People think racism in America is in a word or an image. It isn't. It's in money. The history of our country is that as soon as Black people find a way to build up anything, rich people find a way to take it. Doesn't matter if it's rock and roll, rap, or subprime real estate. They buy it up and bust it from the inside. This country was founded on capitalism, and Black people were the first commodity sold on Wall Street. Now we'll be the first to be stripped of a business that we built, and in exchange some of us will get housing in Wall Street–backed private prisons.

If wholesale prices were going to drop as low as he said, every weed dealer in every city in America was going to be out of a job. It was hard to imagine. I mean, at the time, prices were high and business was boomin'. I was buying at $2,000, selling at $4,000. I was doing great, like *great* sales, selling all over the country: Atlanta, Indiana, Ohio, Michigan, DC, Georgia, New York, Pennsylvania, Florida, and Missouri. You name the place, and I was there.

That $400 price point Josh had just waved at us seemed impossible. Little did I know that it would actually turn out worse than that.

As I write this, in the early Trump years, it costs me more to fill my shitty-ass car with 87 gas than it does to buy an ounce of weed at my price. I've seen wholesale prices as low as $200 a pound. The market is murdered.

And people like me weren't the only ones squeezed. You have people around the country who've been doing this shit for generations. In California, there are people who been up in those hills growing weed for a hundred years.

They're gonna be out too. They just don't all know it yet.

I went home, packed some things, and went on a two-week trip. First I flew from San Francisco to Denver, where I checked in at the Cannabis Cup. I didn't have an entry, but one of my connects was considering going legal and wanted to see the competition. Plus it was a great place to meet more contacts.

His name was Doug and he was another ex-soldier, from Santa Rosa. He and his dad had gone in on a pot-growing operation and they'd spent years developing a bud that had an amazing color. It was so fucking purple that people started calling it Blueberry, or *that Black*.

Blueberry was so deep purple that if you bust the buds open, it looks black. Weed like that is great because you know it's going to be a heavy hitter that's gonna put you to sleep. It was legendary stuff, and he sold almost exclusively to me.

He did it in style too. He delivered his pounds on motorcycles. Sometimes I picked up from him, but it went the other way, he did it cool.

Doug and I had a weird relationship. After we'd make a move, we'd go to the nearest Hooters, sort of as a joke. It wasn't really about looking at the women. We just both really like Hooters' wings. Doug and his dad were doing this to pay for his father's medical bills, so over the course of a dozen or so trips to Hooters eating those probably-toxic wings, his dad basically had his whole intestinal tract removed.

Anyway, Doug was already in Denver when I got there. No longer in the military—he'd served in Afghanistan—his brown curly hair was shaggy and hung down in the back over his camo jacket.

I didn't share any concerns with him, and just made arrangements to make a pickup as usual, in a few weeks. In the meantime, we sampled some of the Cup entrants, including one of the winners, which was called Girl Scout Cookies. It was grown by some people neither of us knew, but it would turn out to be a big hit up and down the coast.

I thought it was okay. Doug thought everything was shit compared to Blueberry.

"B-minus," he said, shrugging.

I flew on to New Orleans, to visit a girlfriend at Loyola—again, things were messed up with Courtney at the time—then flew to DC and on to New York to meet Jerome.

Even though Jerome distributed for me in Detroit, I always met him in New York. We'd meet at the house of a woman who moves major units in NYC who lived in a brownstone on the Upper West Side, a Black lady named Miss Francine, who we called Ole Girl among ourselves.

A long time before, during a brief period when Jerome and I were living in Brooklyn, Miss Francine sold us major work. She was a big-time plug. We called it the taxicab move because we were buying in Manhattan and selling in Brooklyn. Miss Francine had great weed, but I was in California now and other than forgoing the risk of getting it from Cali to NYC, there wasn't much room in terms of price for us to work. But we still met at her place regularly, just to keep that contact fresh.

Jerome had become my most trusted second. It wasn't just that we'd been through a lot. Hell, we'd been shot at together, and he actually had been shot. Also, he never flexed on me, like, "All right, I'm running this shit now."

If I needed something, he always took care of me. He was a very loyal, very humble guy in that way. Whenever I had hard times and I needed him to come through, he came through.

He had interests outside business, in music for instance. He also had a good head on his shoulders, or so I thought.

When we met up in New York, something wasn't right. He started talking about a trip he'd just taken to Vegas. I'd noticed he was going to Vegas more and more, often without telling me. I knew because he'd post photos on Instagram. What self-respecting drug dealer puts geotagged selfies on social media? It worried me, but you can only pull the leash so many times.

Also, he'd started to buy jewelry. Had a new gold chain around his neck, and the nicest, crispiest pair of Jordans on his feet. He wore different shoes on the two days we were together. Like he actually packed two different pairs of brand-new sneakers for an overnight trip to New York.

"Jerome, man," I said. "It's none of my business, but what's with the fashion? You trying to impress someone?"

He shrugged and smiled. "It ain't trickin' if you got it."

I said nothing, then packed up and made preparations to head home. The plan was to get back to Oakland, make a run up to Santa Rosa to stock up on Blueberry, do the Hooters ritual, then re-evaluate.

The only flight back to the Bay Area had a connection through Phoenix. I booked it, cabbed it out to JFK, and started home.

I'd be lying if I said I knew in advance something was wrong. The nature of this thing is that to some degree you're always expecting that tap on the shoulder, that knock on the door. But years can and do pass without real trouble, if you play by the rules.

If anything, my trip had reassured me a little. Logan was the same. Doug seemed the same. Jerome, maybe wobbling a little personally, but basically the same. Maybe I was being paranoid.

I got off the plane in Phoenix, looked up the gate for my connection, started walking that way. I had headphones on and I remember the Wiz Khalifa song—"In Tha Cut."

I was lost in the song when suddenly I noticed, standing up against the wall in the terminal, a scraggly-looking, short-ass white dude with this little Colonel Sanders beard. Just standing there, smiling a little. I couldn't hear him, because I had the music playing, but I saw him reach out and show me some kind of ID.

I ripped my headphones out in time to hear:

"—enforcement agency. Are you Huey Carmichael?"

What in the actual fuck?! OMG! Was this the end?

"Why?"

"Can you come with me, please?"

"Am I under arrest?"

"Not at this time."

I frowned. This didn't make sense. These people are not known for making mistakes when they move. Actually, it's the opposite. They're known for only moving on you when it's too late. How could they hit me without enough for an arrest? Why would they even expose themselves?

I looked at the guy, said nothing, and looked down at my watch.

"What are you doing?" he asked.

I've got a rule: *I watch sixty seconds tick off on my watch before I say anything I might regret.* But fuck that guy if I'm going to tell him about any of my rules. He can read it in this book. I said nothing, watched the second hand move past the 12, then looked up.

"Nah," I said. "I think I'll pass."

I walked away. Didn't look over my shoulder. Didn't wait to see if he followed. I went to the bathroom, erased my main burners, dumped my other burners, and I got rid of mail tracking slips I hung onto. Then went straight to my gate. When I got there, I pulled out my cell phone and made a few phone calls.

Called Courtney, gave her the Spring Cleaning code. What's the Spring Cleaning code? I call someone up and fucking say, "Spring Cleaning." Which means, get rid of anything that looks like evidence, get the shit and the money out the house. You go search through everything, get rid of everything. Paperwork, anything. Plastic—*anything*, everything. This is serious.

Which brings me to a rule: *Plan for the worst.*

I've run the Spring Cleaning drill plenty of times when I had false scares. But this wasn't a drill.

I wasn't thinking straight enough to do much else. An hour later, I was still looking over my shoulder. I had a few minutes before the flight, so I went to a bar and downed three shots of Woodford Reserve neat. When I got on the plane, I kept drinking, heavily. I needed a clear head, but nerves took over I kept thinking: the feds don't fuck up. I can't be clear.

By the time I got off the plane in San Francisco I was good and sloppy. I looked around the terminal. Nothing, except maybe one suspicious looking guy standing at my gate with no bags. Then I walked toward the baggage claim, and goddamn if I didn't see that same Colonel Sanders–looking motherfucker leaning up against the wall in the corridor just before the claim area.

At least I thought it was him. Maybe I was seeing things? I walked by like he was a hallucination, hoping he was, then went down to the carousel, which already had bags tumbling on it. I stared at the fifty yards between myself and that carousel like a condemned man looking at his last corridor.

I decided to stall. I needed a smoke. I walked out of the terminal, pulled out a Turkish Silver, and lit up. Took a long drag—it tasted good—then called Courtney.

"Listen. If I don't call you back in a few minutes, you should be worried. If I'm not in a car headed to see you within ten, it's trouble."

"Okay, baby."

"Let me get back to you."

I walked back into the terminal. It was eerie: there was nobody around the carousel, and practically no one in the whole warehouse-like room. The only people there were these five guys loitering in the same general area, pretending not to know each other. My man Colonel Sanders was part of the five.

Fuck it, I thought, and went to get my stuff.

I had a goddamn hockey bag spinning round there. I reached out and the moment my hand touched it, hell broke loose. They swarmed me like New York pigeons on a piece of bread.

One of them touched my arm. Another touched my hair. It was very intimate, in a negative way.

"Huey Carmichael?" one of them asked.

This time it wasn't the Colonel. The voice belonged to an army-looking guy in a crew cut and one of those too-tight Men's Wearhouse suits those assholes all wear.

"Why?"

"We have reason to believe you're transporting a large amount of drugs or money."

"Well, I'm not."

"Then in that case, you won't mind if we search your bags?"

"Nah. I *do* mind."

"But you said you're not carrying anything."

"I'm carrying my constitutional right to not be searched."

He frowned.

"Okay. Well, let us take these bags, and we're gonna take them to the station, put the dogs on them, and if the dogs hit, then we're gonna search them."

"No. Bring the dogs here. Right now, I'll wait. Or let me go."

"We can confiscate them and deliver them to you. Where do you live?"

"I'm not giving you my address."

They all looked at each other. My mind was racing, trying to figure out what those looks meant. Crew Cut then starts guessing where I live, as in *Do you still live on boom, boom, boom street?*

They fucked up, but still rattled me. The street *number* was right, the street wasn't. They were stumbling and bumbling, but said enough for me to know that they had something.

They were like, "Do you still live here? We'll drop you right off when we're done."

"I'm calling my lawyer," I said.

I dialed my first-ever attorney, a guy who got me out of a little jam when I was a teenager. He was a friend of my father's back in Maryland, an old white dude with prostate trouble named Steven Greenbaum. I gave him a brief outline of what happened, asked for advice.

I loved and trusted Steve. He used to represent the NAACP once upon a time, which is how he knew my father. Their paths had crossed back in the seventies somehow. His rep was that he'd turned down two judgeships to represent poor and mostly Black clients.

He had a quality that I like in a lot of lawyers, a kind of effortlessly nonjudgmental attitude. Like you could tell Steve that you got caught fucking a chicken in the middle of a street, and he wouldn't even blink. He'd make a joke out of it, as in: "A chicken, eh, Huey? Well, we all need hobbies . . ."

So telling him that I was in a crowd of DEA agents at an airport didn't faze him. If anything, he sounded bored. I put him on the phone with the agents.

Crew Cut had a brief talk with Steve, then handed the phone back to me with that pissed-off look cops always get when they talk with lawyers. I *love* that look. My heart slowed to a less life-threatening pace at the sight of that look.

"Listen, Huey," I heard Steve saying on the phone. "They don't have a warrant, but they do have the guns. Do you have anything?"

"Nah."

"Then let them search."

"Okay."

I put my phone in my pocket, folded my arms, and said, "Okay, go ahead."

I opened up my hockey bag. It looked pretty bad. It was packed full—two big vacuum sealers, and the rest was just rows and rows and rows of vacuum seal bags. Not a stitch of clothes. Remember, I was about to head to Santa Rosa.

They were all looking at each other with huge smiles on their faces, acting like they'd hit the fucking jackpot. They're taking out cameras, chuckling, and they're like: "We got you."

"Nah, man, you said *drugs* or *money*. You see any drugs or money in there? No. So get the fuck outta here with all that."

"What are you doing with all these bags?"

"No, no, you got what you need. Now let me outta here."

Crew Cut frowned. They patted me down, took out my wallet. Searched that. Opened my shoulder bag, searched that. Hilariously, they missed a compartment in there that had $3,000 in it, then handed the bag back to me.

They stood there, hands on hips, staring at a hockey bag. Like, they couldn't believe it. Black man with a hockey bag full of plastic bags flying cross-country, and no charge available? Impossible luck.

Had they just been patient, I had moves set up. Like going straight into it. All they had to do was sit back and watch.

Instead they jumped the gun and pulled this bullshit. In hindsight, it was the best thing my government ever did for me.

I picked up the bag, threw it over my shoulder and walked out, triumphant. In a cab, I called Courtney with the good news. Not long after, I got in touch with my man in Santa Rosa, let him know I wasn't coming.

"It's over," I said. "I'm sorry."

"That's okay. I get it. Good luck, Huey."

I went back to my spot in Oakland, had one more Turkish Silver and a beer. Then passed out in my bed, still a free man.

12

Always be shopping (for lawyers).
Dealer-lawyer relationships are like romances. By the time you reach a certain age, you'll have had many of them. They will each mean something different to you. And some memories will be better than others.

In life, in a dark, drunken moment, you might find yourself dialing all your exes in search of a shoulder to cry on. It's the same with lawyers. If you're making moves and shit doesn't add up and things get scary, you'll find yourself calling your lawyers. That's if you're smart enough to have more than one.

I got more than one.

Not long after I got out of college, when I was living in Cincinnati and really struggling, I got in a jam. Well, better to say, my cousin got in a jam.

I was down to scraps that stage in my life. I had maybe $2,000 to my name. I was like a week away from having to live off my actual job salary, and that thought scared the fuck outta me.

I didn't have enough cash to make big deals. I was moving a pound here, a pound there. And things went wrong when I sent a pound to St. Louis, to my cousin Buddy.

We were using FedEx at the time. We had a system. We always requested the "hold for pickup" option, with the idea that the package would show up at a small FedEx storefront.

On the appointed day, the pickup man was supposed to get up way before the storefront opened, and stake out the store.

You're just watching to make sure nobody is setting up behind the counter, no police are going in and out, etc. Then, when the truck arrives with all that day's shit from the airport, you just walk in and say: "Yo, I got *boom boom boom*." Generally they get it, and you walk away.

This gives the package a solid delivery address, a totally clueless person to receive it and keep it safe, and keeps you out of the equation until you (or someone else) comes through to pick it up.

Do that right, maybe you're a few percentage points safer. It's no guarantee, but neither is a condom. Doesn't mean it's not a good idea.

It's my system and I like it. But what does my little cousin do? Why, he fucks it up, of course.

On the day the pound is supposed to arrive, I get at Buddy at like 7:30 a.m., then again at 7:45, and again at 8:00, 8:10, 8-fucking-15. Nothing. I know the FedEx opens at eight. At 8:30 he calls me back and sounds hungover, or stoned maybe. Whatever it was, he was still half asleep.

"Yo, cuz," he says. "My fault, I overslept."

"You *what*? You have one *job* . . . *just one*. If I was the white man, you'd have been up *early* with bells on!"

"What do I do?"

I immediately think of that two grand I have left. A man with a bigger stack can afford to fold this hand. I should walk away. But I don't.

I start calling FedEx. That's the first mistake. I shouldn't call, at least not multiple times. I should call one time, ask them to redeliver, and leave it at that.

For some reason they won't redeliver the package. They're like, "Nah, we can't send it back out. We need you to come and get it."

My neck hairs rise up at this. I know I should just tell Buddy to go and chalk this up to the game. But I don't. I put my foot into his ass and chew him out. I do yell when people veer off script, especially when people fuck up the house's money. I'm learning to stop that.

In fact, I have a habit of yelling and giving speeches when I'm making a wrong decision. Rule: *If you talk long enough to hear yourself giving a speech, you're probably fucking something up.* I'd realize that much later in life. But at the time of this story, I'm in my early twenties and still don't know life.

My approach to Buddy is: "Listen, I have a formula. My formula works. You operated outside of the formula. Now we're in no-man's-land. This shit is your fault. *You* go get it."

So Buddy goes to get it.

He walks to the main FedEx warehouse, stands outside for a minute, takes a deep breath, and goes in. At the desk he politely says his name. The white man behind the counter taps a few keystrokes, then pushes a box forward. He doesn't make eye contact with Buddy, who feels reassured.

He takes the box and makes moves toward the door. Straightaway, all hell breaks loose. The dude behind the counter pulls a badge up from under his neck. "Hold it right there . . ."

My cousin drops the box and breaks toward the exit. This cop leaps over the counter *Starsky & Hutch* style—cops love to act like they're in action movies or TV shows—and barrels toward Buddy, who's stoned or hungover or something and not running fast. (Later I will give him shit about this.)

The cop tackles my cousin, which is bad, but seemingly not too bad. At the time, if my memory is right, the penalty for possession of weed in St. Louis wasn't horrible. It was typically probation under 2,000 grams. Obviously, the crossing-state-lines angle made it worse, but my cousin didn't know that. He thought he was looking at a little weed charge at best.

So he's got this sunburned *Starsky & Hutch* motherfucker on top of him, shoving his face into the tile, and Buddy starts giving up. Why fight it? But as soon as he goes limp, he hears:

"He's going for my gun!"

My cousin freezes. This is before Ferguson, but every Black person in Missouri already knew what it was with cops long before the world decided to take note. Matter of fact, my cousin knew a college student who'd just been shot dead a few weeks before, because he was wearing a red jacket and cops were looking for a guy in a red jacket.

The cop walked. You had a better chance of winning Powerball five times in a row than seeing a St. Louis cop charged in a deadly force case.

All this is going through Buddy's head as he's on the ground and this cop is screaming that he's going for his gun. He shouts back:

"I'm not fighting, I'm not resisting! Don't let him kill me, don't shoot me!"

"He's going for my gun!"

While writhing on the floor of the FedEx office, poor Buddy looks up at a cardboard stand advertising a new set of U.S.

postal stamps that was going to be released, something about "Flags of America." He finds himself staring at an Alaska state flag stamp featuring a badly drawn picture of a whale jumping out of water. The last things I'm gonna see are *stamps*, he thinks. I'm gonna die here!

The cop ends up not shooting my cousin. But Buddy takes a charge. His one phone call goes to a burner phone and word gets back to me over in Cincy. Now I've got to call my Aunt Sonja.

"Again?" she says.

"Yeah."

She sighs hard and heavy. "That boy can't get out of his own way."

Somehow Aunt Sonja never suspects that I'm Buddy's supplier. Or she does, and doesn't want to admit it. That shit always bothered Buddy, but one thing about my cousin: he doesn't snitch, not even to family. So I get to play the good nephew, and Buddy gets to play the disappointing, wrong-path, fuck-up son.

All day long he has to listen to, "Look at how your cousin Huey has a job and works so hard . . ."

But he takes it. He's good like that.

Anyway, Aunt Sonja now asks me to come out to St. Louis. I hop on the next Greyhound and go. Next thing I know, I'm walking through the door of Aunt Sonja's home and already can smell the catfish frying. She's celebrating my arrival, even though her son is about to go away to jail because of me.

I pause to wonder exactly how guilty to feel about that. I quickly realize, to my surprise, that I just don't feel that bad about it, at least not yet. I'm still hotter about Buddy oversleeping. To me, I'm weighing the cost of those extra minutes of sleep against the cost of what is about to come.

Aunt Sonja hugs me, then we sit down to talk. The subject of a lawyer comes up. She says, "I know just the person."

She has a friend, she says, who's just right for the job, a woman named Anita McCall-Jackson. Has an office right around the corner. We can go right now, she's already called.

We go out and walk up the street. On the way, we pass a bench for a bus stop that has a billboard-style ad painted over it. The ad shows a picture of a welcoming, mature-looking Black woman with a broad smile, over the headline:

IN TROUBLE?

Anita can help.

✓ Affordable rates

✓ Specialized felony defense

✓ Domestic violence

✓ Drug crimes

If I represent you, you are family to me.

HIRE THE MOTHER LION!

The picture doesn't look terribly lion-like, but it all sounds right. We walk a block or two, come to a small storefront. I open the door to the sound of a bell. It's an office with cheap plywood paneling, a few file cabinets, and not much else.

There's a young Black female secretary near the door, chewing bubble gum and looking in a mirror, fussing with her hair—even though most of it is wrapped up. She doesn't notice us come in. But Anita herself, a stout woman in a purple suit and black blouse, comes rushing to the front.

"Sonja!" she says, arms extended.

"Anita!"

The two women embrace. I don't know it at the time, but they had been coworkers at the local school where my Aunt

Sonja is an administrator. Actually I do know that; what I don't know is *how* previously they worked together.

But we're coming to that.

Anita leads us to her office, a bigger space in the back of the storefront with a big desk and some chairs. She takes out a yellow legal pad and starts taking notes.

"Okay, tell me everything."

I start telling her the story. The Lioness keeps saying, "Mm-hmm" and writing furiously in her notebook. I'm ten minutes in before I realize she hasn't asked me any questions.

"Anyway," I say, wrapping up, "he's supposedly at the . . ."

I have to unwrap a piece of paper I'd stuffed in my pocket. I read out the name:

"Buzz Westfall Correctional Center. He's there right now. He's going to want to see you right away."

"Buzz . . . Westfall . . . Correctional . . . okay, got it," she says, hitting the final period with the pen for emphasis.

She looks up and smiles. "Well," she says, "I think I can help."

"You do?"

"Yes, of course," she says, smiling. Then she looks over at Aunt Sonja and tells her the retainer is $6,000.

Aunt Sonja sags like she's taken a bullet, but rallies. In reality, I'm going to end up paying this bill, but Aunt Sonja doesn't know that yet. "Of course, Anita," she says. "We'll get that right to you."

Anita gets up and extends a hand. "I'll go see Buddy right away, and then we'll talk again."

We walk out. I've got a funny feeling, but whatever. This is someone my aunt knows. And besides, if I'm going to end up paying money to someone, I want to give a Black lawyer a chance. I especially want to go with a Black woman.

I go right away to the jail and Buddy is freaking out. In addition to the drug charge, they hit him with attempted assault on a police officer and attempted *robbery* of a police officer—to wit, attempting to steal his gun.

"Like I'm gonna steal a cop's gun in the middle of an office full of people!" he shouts. "What am I gonna do, shoot my way out of the city over a fucking *pound?*"

I can tell he's scared, thinking about the years. But I know my cousin won't talk. He's solid like that. It doesn't even enter his mind. He's been busted enough times that he's actually bored with the attempts to flip him. I ask him about that and he laughs.

"They came in here, asking who sent the package and all that, we can help you, blah blah," he says later, aimlessly looking around the meeting room. "I was like, 'Nah, fuck outta here.' And that was it. They just walked out."

I try to calm him down by telling him we've gotten him a lawyer. He nods and I leave.

Anita manages to get bail, even though the number is way too high—Buddy only has minor nonviolent stuff on his sheet. But at least he's out.

We go to see Anita about the case. Her energy level bothers me right away. She seems impatient listening to Buddy telling his story and protesting his innocence.

But when we start talking to her about a plea, I can see right away it gets her pulse moving. Before she gets too excited, I cut in.

"He's willing to do some time, but we don't want it to be any more than a year," I say. "We don't want any felonies. We don't want any drug charges, so he can still get out and maybe go to school someday."

In this country, you can kill a person—hell, maybe more than one person—and still get public housing or a student loan when you get out. But get caught picking up a pound of weed somewhere, and you're done. You're off the grid once you've got a drug conviction. That's why you've gotta try to keep the drug charges out.

She shakes her head. "That's asking a lot, but I'll see what they say."

We come back days later. She's got a big smile.

"I talked to the D.A," she says. "He's willing to go down to five years."

Buddy almost jumps out of his chair.

"Lady," he exclaims, "Are you *smiling* over that shit? The fuck are you thinking?"

At the profanity, Anita gasps and throws a hand over her heart. I glare at Buddy and slide my chair forward to move in between them some, turning my back to him.

"I'm sorry. He didn't mean that," I say. "I think what my cousin is trying to say is . . ."

I smile and start to give a speech, then catch myself as it hits me, too. Did she just say *five years*?

"Fuck this," I say. "What Buddy means is, that's not what we told you to come back with. The only legit charge is the weed. He can do a year, max."

"I don't think they're going to go for that."

"Well, we aren't going for five years. Plus, what do they have? Where is the video? I know I saw cameras in there. I know they have a sign saying, Smile You Are Under Surveillance. Is that only unless you get accused of assaulting a cop? He didn't try to steal the gun. Remember, you work for us!"

"I don't know. I'll ask," she says, rolling her eyes. She actually rolls her eyes, like Buddy's inconveniencing her, trying to get out of sitting in a cage for five years.

Days pass. She calls us, tells us to come in.

We go. This time, she's beaming.

"They're willing to go down to three years!"

Buddy walks out in frustration and comes back in a minute later.

"Three years over a motherfucking *pound*?"

Now she's indignant. "It's not just the drugs, young man," she says. "That officer you fought with, he apparently was very seriously injured, in the shoulder. What do you have to say about that?"

"Look at me. I'm five-eight, maybe 130. That cop is like six-four and built like Andre the Giant. And he tackled me, not the other way around. Whose side are you on?"

"I've got his medical reports, right here. He's got a severely separated shoulder. You must be stronger than you think."

Buddy looks at me, helpless. I shake my head.

"Did you get the video at least?"

"As a matter of fact, I did not. The system was under maintenance that day."

"Of course it was. Look, you really want to be known as the lawyer who got a guy three years in jail for getting tackled? Please, go and come back with something that makes sense. Tell them—"

"No!" she says, sitting up.

She puts her hands on her hips and stares down at us. It's a green suit today and suddenly the whole room feels that color.

"I've done the best I can do. Three years is all you're going to get. It's *not* going to get any better than that."

She turns to Buddy and points a finger at him.

"Son," she says, "you just need to take responsibility for what you did and take this as a lesson learned."

I stare back at her, aghast.

"Son? You're not his *mom*. You're his lawyer." I frown. "How did you say you knew my aunt again?"

"We worked together at R.G. Central Middle."

"You worked at her school. As what?"

"I was a guidance counselor."

Now things are starting to make sense.

"And how long ago were you a guidance counselor?"

"I just opened my practice in March."

I don't even have to count on my fingers.

"But it's only June!"

"I'm a good lawyer."

"Maybe eventually," I say, getting up from the chair.

Buddy follows, grabbing his jacket.

"You fired," he says.

Six thousand dollars. She took that money and ran. What are we gonna do now?

We decide to start asking around the neighborhood, hitting Buddy's corners. At one point we're talking to a guy Buddy knows named Dez, when suddenly we're interrupted.

Two little boys who couldn't have been more than eleven are playing one-on-one on a nearby court. One of them, overhearing, shouts out:

"You need to get that dude who got that guy off who shot that other dude in the head!"

Dez nods. "Oh, yeah. That guy is good."

"Somebody shot someone in the head and this guy got him off?"

"Yeah. My man was in the street, just basically chilling, and then just a little argument transpired, and then dude pushed dude's sister, cause she just was around, and then it was quick from there. The dude drew down and did what he did, in front of like fifteen witnesses."

Everywhere we go, we get the same story: hire the guy who got the guy off for shooting that other guy in the head. Everyone's heard the story, but no one remembers the lawyer's name. The best info we get is that the last name is "Le-Something."

We end up finding an Ed LeBlanc, criminal attorney, in the yellow pages. We call, explain briefly, and make an appointment for the next day.

LeBlanc turns out to be more of a downtown lawyer, in a high rise on Big Bend Road. Fifteenth floor and it's a glass door with embossed gold letters:

EDWARD LEBLANC, Esq.

We go in. An alert and pretty Latina receptionist takes our names and has us fill out a form. She also makes us coffee. Neither of us drink coffee, but we take the cups and pretend to drink. Five minutes later, we meet LeBlanc.

He's a tall man with slicked-back blond hair, in a tie, shirt-sleeves, and blue slacks. The matching blue suit jacket rests on a hanger on the doorknob. There's photos of him on the wall with all sorts of liberal luminaries—Dick Gephardt, Claire McCaskill, and Richard Trumka from the AFL-CIO, but also Jesse Jackson, Johnnie Cochran, Benjamin Crump, etc. I wonder if he puts those last photos up just for the Black clients.

He puts his feet up on the desk.

"So, stealing a cop's gun? That sounds like bullshit."

The word *bullshit* is like a breath of fresh air to us both. I look over at Buddy, who smiles ear to ear.

"Yeah. Listen, before we start—is it true you got a guy off for shooting a guy in the head?"

"Shooting a guy in the head . . . Oh, yeah, I remember that case. Tory Boyd, right?"

"I guess. You got him off?"

"*Off?* Fuck no. Tory's up at Farmington right now, doing a nickel."

"Oh."

"But he was looking at thirty."

We shrug and tell Buddy's story. As my cousin describes the plea offers, LeBlanc writhes in his chair like a man suffering from a rattlesnake bite. He flips when we tell him about the "take responsibility" line.

"She said *what?* Well, we'll get that fixed. Give me a day, okay?"

Next thing we know, we're at a motion hearing and LeBlanc is reaming the arresting officer. He has obtained the guy's entire medical history, not just the recent report the D.A. had sent over.

He's like: *Isn't it true,* Officer Murphy-or-whatever, that you've had a separated shoulder since 1992? That you hurt it playing golf and that it's been popping in and out ever since?

The cop says nothing. Long story short, LeBlanc got my cousin a year, with the drug charges wiped out, and everything we originally wanted. And Buddy never overslept again. More than that, he did a whole year rather than speak my name. From then on, I knew I could trust him.

As for LeBlanc, he became my go-to advisor on everything. He had a way of cutting away all the bullshit and getting me to focus on the key problem.

That's why I call him now, after the Arizona debacle. From my house in Oakland, I dial and tell him the rough outlines of my troubles. But something's wrong. He's different on the phone, distant.

"Listen, Huey. It's great to hear from you and all, but I'm not sure I can advise you on this one."

"Why?"

"When was the last time you were in St. Louis?" he asks, irrelevantly.

I say nothing.

"I wish I could hop in a car and come out to talk to you," he continues. "But I've got so much on my plate. Maybe you could come visit me sometime."

Minutes later, my mind races over the call. That was my most trusted and straightforward lawyer, sounding completely mysterious. What exactly did LeBlanc just say, really?

After a bit, I work it out. He's suggesting that I visit St. Louis. And he's suggesting that I drive (*"I wish I could hop in a car . . ."*) instead of fly.

I get in my car and head to St. Louis.

*

I arrive at Aunt Sonja's door two days later. She's expecting me, but there's no big smile this time. No catfish either.

Suddenly, I'm not the good nephew anymore.

Buddy comes over and something is clearly wrong. He's got his head down. One look in his eyes and I guess everything. But he says it anyway.

"Huey, I got popped on that run."

"But you're out."

"Huey, we gotta talk."

A few hours later, I'm in an office with Buddy and LeBlanc. By then Buddy had told me the real story. He'd been stopped just over the border in Missouri by state police working with the DEA. They threatened him with a lot of years, but in the space of hours let him walk away from all those pounds in his trunk. That was with a promise to cooperate.

In a moment of weakness, he'd agreed. But he'd since changed his mind and decided to come clean to me. He says:

"I'm willing to do the time. And I won't testify."

LeBlanc interrupts:

"We've got a good chance to beat it anyway. It was a bad stop. They said he swerved, but I got the dashboard cam footage, and he clearly doesn't. We can beat this."

"Okay."

"But you've got bigger problems, Huey," LeBlanc says. "They know about you."

"That's right," my cousin says.

They were waiting for him on that border. Wasn't a random stop.

What the *fuck*? Who could have known about that? It was such a small list of people who were even possible suspects, I didn't know what to think.

Buddy and I made up—he was relieved almost to tears to be back in the light—and we went back to Aunt Sonja's, where we tried and tried, without success, to figure it out.

Later that night, I called up Steve Greenbaum in Maryland. He was nonjudgmental as always.

"You trust your cousin?"

"I do."

"It sounds like he's in good hands. It's you I worry about."

"Shit, me too."

"I don't mean that. You'll probably beat this. It sounds like they missed their shot. I'm more worried about you as a person."

"What do you mean?"

"Huey, you obviously have to do what's best for you. But if you had to get out, what would you do? If you had to walk out, what could you walk out to? Is there anything?"

Yeah, I thought. There actually is something.

I'd been preparing for this day. The get-out day. And I knew where I wanted to get to.

13

Get to the point.

In February 2004, I was just a kid, living in Cincinnati, Ohio, grinding it out. I was selling a pound here, a pound there, and working double shifts at a Marriott in town.

My apartment was a studio, $350 a month. It was maybe the size of a couple of refrigerators. I used the closets to start my first weed grow. Made shit on it, to be honest. (Like I said before, I've never been a good grower.) But that's how I was living. I was hustling, really hustling, working a lot, Just trying to eke through. I put in a ton of hours at the Marriott, and the best part of the job is that I had health insurance.

I was making twelve dollars an hour, working a solid forty hours a week, usually with overtime. Waiting tables was my full-time job. I was also working as a doorman, and also bartending. I did everything at that place.

The hotel at the time had this really shitty-ass executive lounge. It was called something like the "VIP Center" or the "Restoration Area." The title made it sound like a place you'd wake up in after minor surgery, or greet mourners after a wake. And it almost looked like that too. It was one small plywood bar, a piece of wall-to-wall carpet, and an overhead light.

They tasked me with cleaning it up, gave me a little budget. And I raised up that sad-ass little room into something real. I don't want to say it was world class, because it wasn't world class. But it was damn sure the best executive lounge that I could make.

A bunch of Marriotts are famous as fuck. The Marriott in Cincinnati, it's practically a museum. They're all art deco, Seventies works of art, with beautiful, Brazilian redwood furnishing.

You can't even get that shit anymore. They had the bars made up and the walls done up with artwork and high-arching, vaulted ceilings.

I made the executive lounge match what you walked into. Before, it was just drywall and a TV. And I changed the name, made it the "Biltmore Lounge" because I knew the beat-down, mid-level executive types who stay at Marriotts all have fantasies of being Rockefellers or Vanderbilts. That was clever shit for a kid in his early twenties.

Suddenly guests were using the lounge. It made money. We were restocking booze twice as fast. Soon that alone paid for the improvements.

Then it came time for my salary to be reviewed. Twelve dollars an hour was pretty good for Cincinnati back then. But I'm not like most Americans, who are grateful for whatever crumbs get thrown their way. When I work, I expect to be paid.

Rule: *When you do any work, no matter how menial, always find out exactly how much you're worth. Because someone will always try to pay you less.*

I had added value, and expected to be compensated. But my supervisor, this guy named Mr. Moss—nobody even knew his first name, and there came a time when I began to wonder if he even had one—sat me down and gave me the "good" news.

"Huey, we're really happy with what you've been doing around here," he said. "We're offering you a 3 percent raise."

Huh? A 3 percent raise on twelve bucks? I don't even know what the fuck that looks like, but I started doing the math in my head at that point, and that shit was insulting.

The max, I knew, was 4 percent. They didn't even give me that! I was livid. I thought: I don't want to live like this. I'd brought that lounge from slummin' to one of the jewels of the whole business. Fuck 3 percent.

"Okay," I said to Moss, starting to get up.

"Wait, aren't you going to say 'thank you'?"

"Thank you." I said, and walked out.

I went into the employee locker room, seething, and changed my clothes. I was in waiter garb, had to change into my bartender costume, a costume I'd designed. Hotel bartenders had worn these silly maroon polo shirts that looked like something a server in a sports bar would wear. For the Biltmore room, I made the standard a black brocade vest.

Those were cool. But that day, I felt defeated and pissed. It got worse when I headed toward the lounge for the night shift, and saw Moss scurrying home at five sharp—motherfucker *never* worked late—and crossing the parking lot to get into his tacky "shale metallic" Cadillac XLR.

Who drives a *gray* Cadillac? Something about that bothered me.

I went up to the lounge and wiped down the bar. I had some autonomy in there, but there were also rules. Like unless the customer asked otherwise, the TV always had to be on CNN.

Lately, all day and night, I'd had to listen to news about the presidential election. This was 2004, remember, and we were just weeks shy of Super Tuesday, which included the Ohio primary. For some reason that I neither grasped nor cared about much at the time, Ohio was supposed to be more important than other states. I distinctly remember John King standing in front of a map, saying something like, *Well, Wolf, here's why we give more of a shit about Ohio* . . .

Early that evening, I remember I saw a segment featuring a politician I'd never knew much about, John Edwards. He was standing in front of a public school not far from where I lived, in a Black neighborhood, and he was talking about how we live in "two Americas," one for the rich, and one for the poor.

"We have thirty million people who live in poverty in this country," he was saying. "We have one set of institutions and services for the very wealthy and the special interests, and another set of institutions for the very poor. That isn't right. To live up to this country's promise, we need to address these cultural and societal challenges."

I raised an eyebrow. Now, we remember John Edwards today for ending up in that trash-ass situation, where he got another woman pregnant. I think maybe even in the beginning he tried to say she was lying. Shit, he got a woman pregnant while his wife had cancer. And she fucking *died*. It doesn't get much more fucked up.

But at the time, he was talking about being an advocate for the poor, which is something you don't hear anybody saying to this day. Listen close: politicians will say they're for the middle class, or on the outside they'll say they're for working people. But saying you're for the poor, *nah*.

Edwards saying all this caught my attention because, at the time, I was basically poor. I lived in the hood and I was seeing how people that live right on the other side of downtown, in the commercial district, were making predatory zoning laws. They were fucking the people over in downtown Cincinnati. I was becoming aware.

So this interested me, mildly. But only mildly. Mostly, I was pissed about Moss's Cadillac and my little raise.

I worked a standard shift, busy-ish, hustled some tips. By eleven or so it was slowing down to the end-of-the-bar drinkers—there are always a few in every hotel. On a break earlier I'd worked through my anger a little by smoking a J in the lot, so in the after-hours I was just zoning, wiping glasses down on autopilot, letting the day recede pleasurably, like a tide.

Suddenly, who walks into the Biltmore lounge, but *John Fucking Edwards*. He's staying in the hotel! He looks massacred with exhaustion and some other despair-like emotion I don't recognize. He's trailed by three young people in suits, two men and a woman.

"Vodka tonic, double," he says sharply.

Then he whips his head sideways to look at one of his aides, as if saying, *What?* Like this had been an issue before.

None of the aides say a thing. Nobody wants a drink.

I bring Edwards his double and drop back, keeping a polite distance. I don't make out any words, but the basic vibe of the meeting is, they want to talk, and he wants them to fuck off.

Soon, within minutes, they do. He's alone, crouching over the bar. Nobody in the place recognizes him.

He taps on the bar twice—another double. I come by with the drink. Setting it down, I can see he's got pieces of what look like masking tape on the inside of his suit jacket, probably for where the microphone went. He'd been on TV.

I'm stoned out of my mind and I look up at him, which is a mistake. His face is caked with TV makeup. He's *orange.*

He frowns. "What?"

"I heard you on TV today. That was interesting, about the poor."

He shrugs. "Yeah, well, not according to my staff."

He asks my name. I tell him, I'm Huey Carmichael.

"Like Huey Newton *and* Stokely Carmichael?"

"Yeah."

"Cool name."

He takes a big gulp of vodka and shakes his head.

"Huey, you know why I'm not gonna win this election? Because Americans watch *Lifestyles of the Rich and Famous.* They don't watch 'Lifestyles of the Poor and Fucked.' You understand? I depress people."

"*Lifestyles of the Rich and Famous* was canceled like ten years ago."

He's not listening. He's staring off in another direction, at another corner of the bar, where a group of men and women are sitting. He turns back.

"Huh? Sorry, I was distracted."

"That's okay."

"Where's the bathroom here? I gotta take a shit."

I tell him, down the hall. He gets up, peels off some bills, and drops them on the bar.

"Later," he says.

*

Nearly four years later, maybe December 2007. I'm still in Cincinnati, but things have changed. I've made my Vancouver connect and I'm making money, like real money.

I have Cincinnati and a bunch of other cities sewed up. I still work out the same hotel, too, only now all the service people are dealing for me. By this point I'm taking regular trips to Vancouver, squeezing that shit when I have time. Maybe once a month I'm going up there for three days, then shipping back product.

I've also moved since 2004. I live now in a section called OTR, or Over-the-Rhine. It's a historically Black neighborhood. Well, it used to be German, and then Black. Now, today, it's extremely gentrified. You wouldn't recognize OTR right now. But at this time, I know it.

I'm on my way home one day and I notice something out of place. A storefront that had been empty, all of a sudden there's somebody in there.

Keep in mind, even though I come from where I come from, I'm really a street guy. I don't mean *street* like I'm a thug, but I move around in the street. It's my business to know who's doing what, among other things because I'm selling a lot of weed up and down the block. I know everyone: lawyers, architects, club owners, everybody.

I networked the fuck out of Cincinnati; I *killed* Cincinnati.

So one day I'm on my way home—I live on Main Street in OTR—and I see this new storefront. The sign above the door says, "Center for Dynamic Change."

I walk in and say, "What have y'all got going on here?"

A tall, geeky-looking white dude in a sweater-vest and glasses comes forward.

"Hi. I'm Giles."

"What is this, Giles?"

There's a second question implied in there, but he's too slow to pick up that I'm asking not just what he's doing, but what he's doing in *my neighborhood*. He says:

"Well this is an incubator for, uh, people of color that want to be involved in politics."

What the fuck, I think, is an incubator? I look around.

"More or less the only person of color I see in the office right now is me."

"Are you interested in politics . . .?"

"Huey."

"Are you interested in politics, Huey?"

"I'm not *uninterested* in politics."

"Would you like to get involved?"

"Get involved with what?"

We sit down. He explains that his organization is funded by a consortium of local labor unions, and that they're engaged in a human rights campaign, and they're looking for, uh, people of color to join up with a "fellowship."

"A fellowship, like a paid fellowship?"

Giles nods. "It pays five dollars an hour. But Huey, we'd need a resume before you'd qualify for the fellowship."

I try not to laugh. At that time, I'm probably making between $70,000 to $80,000 a month. I wonder: who can afford to work for five bucks an hour? What a crazy country.

But shit, I'm bored. And understand, I'm interested by then in the concept of political organizing. I want to understand how it works. Some people are mechanical and have uncontrollable urges to take radios and toasters and shit apart, just to see how they work.

I like to take organizations apart, look at them from all sides, see what works and what doesn't. And I like the idea of learning how to change the political scene.

Anyway I go home, scramble to put together a resume—it's all service jobs—and come back. He hires me on the spot, beginning my career in politics.

The group's campaign, it turns out, is about something I frankly don't give a fuck about at the time, LGBTQ rights. It's not that I'm anti, I just never think about it.

Giles, myself, and a bunch of other "fellows" end up being whisked away to a union conference in Michigan to be trained on the subject.

They give us worksheets, where we're tested on what we know about certain terms. Like we have to match the term in column A to the correct answer in column B.

I look down at these sheets and I'm like, "What *is* this?"

You're supposed to match words like *heterosexism* to phrases like, "The belief that heterosexual relationships are better or more normal than queer relationships and people."

Where I grew up, *queer* is a slur, so I check the wrong box. Later, I will catch shit for this. Terminology, I will learn, is a fixation of the college-educated white people who've dreamed up this campaign.

I keep going.

One column says something like, *"Fag/Dyke/etc."* I match that to something that reads like:

Terms which some people have chosen to reclaim despite their history of hurtfulness but which may be oppressive when used by people outside the community.

I can already imagine, they're gonna send me into Black neighborhoods and try to sell this. And I know it won't fly.

I don't think knowledge is bad. I just think that the act of acquiring it can have a separating effect. Every level of education you achieve drives you deeper and deeper into an elite group that's walled itself off like all groups do, with its own language and tribal rituals. The difference with educated people is they think they're above this, when actually they're the most tribal of all. It's fucking sad.

But in this case, I don't say anything. I can see these people are organized and, to a degree, know what they're doing. They're working toward making gay marriage legal, and they have a whole military-style outreach strategy to get there.

Again, if I cared more, I'd have been impressed. In fact I will later take some of their lessons in building my own organization. Rule: *In any big operation, don't weigh your foot soldiers down with too many different orders. Work hard to focus on a few simple goals.*

For instance, they have a strategy for how to get white voters turned around on gay marriage. The approach is: "Gay people, come out to your families. They need to know that there's a gay person in every single family, and you're out of the closet."

The emphasis is on making sure people in white families know they've all got gay relatives. Get that done, you can move on to the legislative part maybe. It's simple and elegant. I like the tactics.

Of course, with Black folks, on this one you can't just go in and be like, "Come out." You know? Because the choir director ain't coming out, not in the middle of church. Everybody knows the choir director in most Black churches is gay, but with us it's hush-hush, be quiet about it. "Transgender" isn't even a thing that you really can talk about. Like even just the word "transsexual" isn't something that you could say in a normal situation.

These tactics, I know straightaway, they're not gonna land in my neighborhood. I'll have to come up with something different. That might even involve learning to care. I had time to work on that.

After the first day of the seminar, a bunch of us are chilling at the bar where we're staying, a hotel in Lansing. We have this pretty redhead who worked with us, a girl named Angie. She's from Seattle. Typical hippie all the way, who wears shoes with rubber bottoms, and cork in between the feet and the bottom, and overalls and a white t-shirt. She was like—you could see her sitting with her feet hanging off a dock in a river.

Pretty hippie girl, what can I say? She's one of the new canvassers. All the guys in the group love them some Angie. She's sitting with us now, flirting with me a little, but nothing serious.

But Giles comes over to sit with us, and I can see right away that he has a more serious thing for her. He keeps looking over protectively, and he's shooting me funny looks the whole time. On top of it all, I soon see he's finishing his beers too fast for a guy who probably doesn't drink much. His mood is heading in the wrong direction.

At one point, whatever it is we're talking about, he interrupts and starts in on me: "So, Huey, what do you think of the seminar?"

"It's okay."

"Did you understand the part about *heterosexual privilege*?"

"Yes."

"You don't seem convinced."

"I got it."

It gets silent at the table.

I frown and decide to turn in, telling everyone I'm tired. To pay for everyone's drinks, I reach into a pocket, pull out a roll of hundreds, and drop one on the table.

I turn my back on the group and, walking away, wave goodnight with the back of my hand. In a wall mirror I can see Giles picking up the C-note and frowning. Think about *that*.

When we get back to Cincinnati, it's time to do the actual outreach.

I have to work out my own feelings. It comes down to a battle of just asking myself, "Do I need to even take an opinion on this?"

I realize: *I don't care who straight people fuck. Why do I care who anyone else fucks?*

This became my line.

I was a huge asset for them. Being a straight Black guy, a masculine straight Black guy, I could walk into places with Black people and actually talk about this shit.

And ten years ago, sure, there'd be homophobic conversations. You know how in white families, everyone's got a racist uncle somewhere? You understand what the hell he's saying— you might not agree, but you understand it. It may not be coming from a bad place, but it's still bad.

I had the authority to walk into these spaces, confront that, and people would be like, "All right, this isn't just gay people care about this. Even this straight guy who's from around here, who we know has beautiful women, talks about this shit."

And my take was, "Why the fuck do you care?"

That wasn't the most rah-rah pro-LGBTQ position, and wasn't within a mile of the union workshop technique. But I was doing what worked.

Looking back, I was using people's homophobia against them. I'd walk into a place and hear someone saying the word "faggot," and I'd just jump on that. Be aggressive, like: "All right. Why do you care who the next person's fucking? What's the deal with that?"

It was confrontational. It wasn't even *Leave them alone!* or *They can love who they want!* or *Lead with love!* or any of that. It was like, "What's this creepy-ass obsession you have? Why is it even occupying space in your head? Is there something you need to talk about?"

That might not have been right. In fact it might even have been the opposite of what they wanted me to do. But it worked.

Or: sometimes, because the church is such a big thing in our communities, people would come at me with, "Because the Bible says—"

And I'd be like, "Nah, *fuck you!*" Say it loud like that. "*Fuck* what the Bible says! There's more shit out here to be worried about, right? So why do you care about this? Why is that even a thing?"

Sometimes they'd send volunteers with me. White kids, from U Cincinnati or Xavier or whatever. They'd see me dropping F-bombs, and they'd be frozen silent, afraid to say a word.

Beyond that, because I had money, I drove a BMW to work. So I was driving all these kids around canvassing in a new 328xi, a convertible, black sapphire in color, a beautiful ride. And I was supposed to be making five dollars an hour. It was hilarious.

It was especially funny since I knew all of this was getting back to Giles, who was too much of a pussy to say anything to me about it.

Things between Giles and me deteriorated quickly. Things took a really serious turn when I started fucking Angie. I wasn't lording it over him or anything, but he knew. So he started giving me a hard time, looking for ways to assert authority.

The first thing that got me in trouble was the donations. We had a rule for fellows: if you were hitting doors, you had to get something like two donations of five dollars per day.

I didn't care about donations. I was just interested in the challenge of the work. So I'd have all these volunteer canvasser kids in tow, and we'd knock on doors, and I wouldn't even ask folks for money. How am I gonna go into a poor neighborhood and ask some old Black lady for five dollars she doesn't have?

So I just paid the quota myself. It worked out probably that I ended up paying to do the job. But what was money? I didn't care. And I didn't think Giles would care, either. He got his money, right?

Wrong.

"Huey," he says to me one day, as I'm walking out. "It's come to my attention that you're not asking for donations."

"I'm meeting the quota, ain't I?"

"Not with donations."

"What's the difference?"

"We're training people for political work. Like it or not, it's important that these young people learn how to ask for money."

"Okay."

I start to walk out, going slowly enough to offer him the opportunity to stop and say some more shit, if he has more to say. He doesn't. He's biting his lip so hard it looks like it might bleed.

After that day, I'm pissed. Also, I have to make a run to Vancouver. I go, and Kermit and I get to partying, and there's some delays. It's nothing serious, but I end up not making it back to Cincinnati for a while, like eight days.

I could call Giles. But I don't. I just don't feel like it.

On the ninth day, I walk back into the office. Giles bolts out of his chair and hurries over. He's like, "You've been gone nine days. I got to fire you."

I'm like, "No, I need the job."

"Huey, I'm firing you."

I say nothing, go out to my car, pull a half-ounce out of a false compartment I've got behind the radio panel, and come back to the office. I set the half-ounce on his desk, and say, "Here."

I don't know how I knew he smoked, but I knew. I was not fired that day.

There's a dynamic that happens once people find out you're a dealer, or even just that you've got access to drugs. The chemicals in their brains change. You're like Obi-Wan Kenobi in *Star Wars*. I'm fired? Fuck outta here. You can go about your business.

And they do, they just fuck right off.

After that, I did and did not come into work as I pleased. And even though, looking back, I was a terrible employee in multiple respects, I was about all they had to show for minority recruitment.

It was so bad on that front that I even earned a visit from a hotshot higher-up from the union office in DC, a Black guy named Anderson Dixon. He'd been some kind of big organizer in the sixties, and because Giles mentioned he'd finally recruited an effective young Black fellow, this Dixon guy came out to meet me.

Literally sight unseen, Dixon seeks me out in the office, Giles in tow, and puts his arm around me. It's an accident I'm even at work that day. Worse, I'm high as a kite and reek of Kermit's tree. My eyes are red as maraschino cherries. I have to put in Visine just to meet the man.

Nonetheless, he gets his arm around me and says: "Huey, Giles here has told me all about you. You have great potential. You could go a long way. I'm really excited."

He pats me on the back and walks out, after giving me a line about fast-tracking me. It's really sad. I feel guilty and used at the same time.

As that year progressed, this interesting thing happened. I remember initially I had been following Edwards, because he was running again that year. I always remembered that he talked about the poor, and had taken a shit in my executive lounge.

But then also Barack Obama was running that year. And honestly, I didn't take him seriously at first.

This was the reality of my world. Imagine you're in a tall building with a balcony. Your reality is, if you jump off this motherfucking balcony, you're going to die.

The same sort of rule applied to my certainty that there would never be a Black president. It was just that cut and dried. Everyone felt that way where I lived.

You could walk down the street and ask the first Black person you saw, "When you were born, did you think that you would see a Black president in your lifetime?" And I promise you, the answer would have been no, across the board.

And so for me, I experienced a big change that year when Obama won the South Carolina primary. It was like stepping off that balcony and floating. Like, this is a new world now, I can *fly*. I was like, "Okay, Huey, you should do this."

Remember, until then I was basically doing this weird-ass hobby working for the union, canvassing on gay rights issues mainly because there's a lot of downtime in being a drug kingpin. I had other interests, why shouldn't I explore? But none of it really came from a place of idealism.

That changed when Obama's candidacy jumped in front. I gradually dropped the union campaign and went to work for a regular Obama field office once he'd sewed up the nomination.

I didn't like the way they ran their offices. There are certain ways you are and are not supposed to treat employees. I knew this from my own business. In their case, if volunteers come into your office, you shouldn't walk them straight to a desk, sit them down, and give them a list of phone numbers to call.

There's a level of engagement that's supposed to take place in any workplace, for several reasons. You don't want them to feel used, because you want them to keep coming back. You don't want bad word-of-mouth, either.

Just like in my world, your best advertisement is person-to-person. People learn you treat your people well, they'll work hard for you, show loyalty.

And the Obama offices I went into just didn't feel good. They'd sit me down and walk away. I'd literally get up and turn around and leave, and nobody as much as had my phone number to keep in contact with me, or even notice that I was gone.

Still, I campaigned in my own way. I was still making runs north, and I would take a bunch of Obama pins and buttons and I'd give them away.

Border guards loved that shit, man. The Canadian border guards, I mean. I'd give them all this merch, and it was a lot of love, because Obama was like a rock star at the time. I just remember how funny it was. Here I am, making these drug runs and campaigning for Obama internationally at the same damn time.

I remember, when I first heard Sarah Palin's name, I was in Sioux City, South Dakota. I remember waking up that morning, turning on NPR, and getting ready to ride out from Sioux City to Missoula, Montana—that was my next stop.

That whole day, they were talking about Sarah Palin, where she was from, what her weird fucking deal was. I remember crossing the border, handing out a box full of HOPE buttons, and by the time I got to Vancouver, the news was official that she was the running mate. Then I re-upped with Kermit.

Politics was very much intertwined with what the fuck I was doing during this time.

I remember being in Vancouver on that trip and feeling bad that I'd soured things with Giles and the union. I didn't *need* to show up the little motherfucker. Maybe I could have contributed more.

That was a bittersweet week. The world felt like it was changing, but for the first time, I had some reservations about my lifestyle. I remember driving out from Vancouver to Toronto with the load, thinking about all kinds of shit. After connecting with Vihaan and sending him south toward the Windsor checkpoint with our load, I remember, I spent a whole day thinking about my future. Was this what I really wanted to do with my life?

Maybe not, I thought. Hope and change and all that. Yeah, I fell for that shit, too.

I still did end up contributing that year, in my own way. I donated the max to Obama and wrote some checks for other political causes, the Human Rights Campaign included.

I learned to cut lots of small donation checks: nine hundred bucks here, a thousand bucks there, to local candidates. Some of these have actually risen up in the ranks of Ohio politics since.

I remember once that fall, I bought a ticket to a high-dollar congressional fundraiser, just to have a place to take Courtney. She was always in and out of my life and was very into that sort of thing, especially that year—she wanted to *be* Michelle Obama.

And an aide to the guy I was donating to, he pulled me aside at that dinner and said, "Where you from?"

"Jersey, originally."

"Man, you just seem like a really big fish in a small pond out here. You'd do well if you stayed."

What could I say? Nothing, really. But it made me think. Maybe someday, I thought. Maybe I could do this for real.

Now, almost eight years later, it seemed that *someday* might be here. I was going to have to leave my other life. Could political work be a future?

Yeah, I thought, it could be. But I had to get there first. I had to get out from under the net.

14

Get your money and get out.

After getting approached by the feds, I got so low I started to
break my own rules, including: *Never put anything down on paper
you wouldn't want to see on the front page of the* New York Times.
This applies to unencrypted digital communication as well.

I'd followed that one for decades. Well, fuck that now. I
took out a yellow legal pad, pulled out my phone and a lap-
top, and began making a handwritten list of events with
corresponding dates.

Didn't even bother to use code. I had an ashtray right next
to the pad and was going to burn that motherfucker as soon as
I was done. The first pass looked something like this:

Dec 5, 2015 Josh and Sally reveal, harvest fucked
Dec 12 Mtg at lab. Arrange sending loads east for L, J, J
Dec 15 Send first load out (ATL)
Dec 19 Second load (NY)
Dec 22 Third load (College Park)
Dec 27 Fourth load goes out (STL)
Dec 29 911 from Reece re B
Dec 30 911 from B (bet KC & STL)
Dec 29?–Jan 2? Josh out yachting with Wall Street guys

Feb 8–9 2016 Lawrence hit (BAL)
Feb 10 Fight w Courtney
Feb 11 Meet w Lawrence

March 18 Mtg w Josh, who announces—he's out

April 15 Meet Doug at Cannabis Cup
April 16–22 NOLA (Tina)
April 24–25 Meet Jerome (NY)
Apr 26 JFK-Pho (Feds!!!)
Apr 26 Pho-SFO (Feds!!!)
Apr 27 Call LeBlanc. He tells me (?) to drive to STL
Apr 29 Arrive STL. B confesses, he's been hit. Meet w LeBlanc & B

I stared at the paper. It was now a week after the last events: June 6, 2016. I fiddled with the list, adding asterisks on problem dates. I also added some earlier episodes going back in time. I'd lost a small shipment of ten pounds about a year before involving an old college friend I worked with down there, a funny little dude named Kevin Gleeson, who I just called "K."

Lawrence had been hit in November of 2015. My girlfriend Tina's cousin in New Orleans, a kid named Corbin who worked for me there, had been hit in the summer, in August, losing five pounds. But he was a stand-up kid, a young g, and, true to the rules, he ate the loss as a gift to me. As in: *Always pay the plug.*

Jerome meanwhile had been hit a long time before, at the beginning of 2015. He'd only been hit twice, once in the previous year, and once after my last Canada run—twice in eight years. That's a pretty clean record in this business.

But all of this was normal. In fact, when I looked back, I'd been losing product pretty steadily for years. It was never enough to be noticeable. But four, five times a year, I'd lost shipments or had other things go wrong.

There was no pattern to any of it.

After multiple passes and revisions, the final list from the last eighteen months or so looked something like this:

March 2015 Jerome 5 (DET) *
May 2015 K 10 (ATL) *
August 2015 Corbin 5 (NO) *
November 11 Lawrence (BAL) * Not lost—SHORT!!!

Dec 5, 2015 Josh and Sally reveal, harvest fucked
Dec 12 Mtg at lab. Arrange sending loads east for L, J, J
Dec 15 Send first load out (ATL)
Dec 19 Second load (NY)
Dec 22 Third load (College Park)
Dec 27 Fourth load goes out (STL)
Dec 29 911 from Reece re B *
Dec 30 911 from B (bet KC & STL) *
Dec 29?–Jan 2? Josh out yachting with Wall Street guys

Feb 8–9 2016 Lawrence hit (BAL) * SHORT AGAIN!
Feb 10 Fight w Courtney
Feb 11 Meet w Lawrence

March 18 Mtg w Josh, who announces—he's out

April 15 Meet Doug at Cannabis Cup
April 16–22 NO (Tina)
April 24–25 Meet Jerome (NY)
Apr 26 JFK-Pho (Feds!!!)
Apr 26 Pho-SFO (Feds!!!)
Apr 26 Tell Doug I'm out
Apr 27 Call LeBlanc. He tells me (?) to drive to STL
*Apr 29 Arrive STL. B confesses, he's been hit. Meet w LeBlanc & B **

None of this made sense. There wasn't one person on the list who knew all the other people. I was the only common factor, and I damn sure wasn't snitching on myself.

You could imagine the government had some space-age surveillance thing looking at everything I did. But if that was the case, why was I walking and breathing free? Why didn't they hit me when I was carrying duffel-bags full of tree into Courtney's building? Hell, why hadn't they hit her place?

It didn't add up. The conversation with Buddy in St. Louis absolutely confirmed that the Feds not only knew about me, they knew enough about me to hit Buddy with a trunkful of pounds.

But they were somehow still ignorant enough to not know where I stored my loads, or where all my routes were. Also, I noted that some of my newer contacts had never been messed with. I'd never had a problem with Doug, for instance. None of my "foreclosure grows" had ever been hit.

Moreover, a few of my older contacts, like white boy Charlie from Maryland—he was still selling weed at the University at College Park, all these years later—he'd never been hit either.

But I'd only started doing business with Charlie again recently, since I'd started selling Doug's Blueberry. I'd guessed correctly that Charlie's rich college clients, always the worst snobs when it comes to weed, would eat that product up. So we'd reconnected in late 2014.

There, and in maybe a half-dozen other places, I'd never had a problem. But how was that possible, if someone knew enough about me to pull me off a goddamn plane with a big-ass hockey bag, packed full of food-saver bags?

I stared at the paper for an hour, trying to find a pattern. Finding none, I tore the sheet off the pad, rolled it into a cone of paper, flicked a lighter below, and watched it burn. For good measure I burned the blank pages underneath.

I doubted police actually used that pencil-rubbing trick, but who knew? Cops watch movies too. Matter of fact, they watch too many. It's why I was never sure if body cameras were a good idea. Having cops be cops is bad enough. Having them be cops and wannabe stars of screen, even worse.

Sighing, I stood up, went over to my cabinet and pulled out a baggie of Doug's purplest bud. I rolled one and sat on the couch, smoking till my brain went numb. Blueberry fucks you up, man. The high sat on me like a boulder.

Sleepily, I tuned to the TV. Out of a habit probably left over from my Marriott days, my TV was permanently turned on CNN. As the screen popped on I was immediately met with an image of presidential candidate Donald Trump at a lectern in Redding, California.

He was wearing his trademark MAKE AMERICA GREAT AGAIN cap, only the color scheme was off. It wasn't red and white, but a camouflage hat with orange letters.

I frowned. Was the hat real, or a Blueberry-induced neurological mistake? I burst out laughing, mainly at the memory that *Donald Trump* was about to be the Republican nominee. I'd forgotten somehow. I'd also forgotten, the California primary was the next day. Trump was always babbling some crazy shit. I wondered what it was, and turned up the volume:

...there's an African American guy who is a fan of mine. Great fan, great guy! You know what I'm—look at my African American over here!

And he pointed. My jaw dropped in awe, and my brain locked up. As was often the case with Trump, one hemisphere said to laugh, while the other was infuriated.

Next thing I knew, the footage cut off, and they cut back to a studio, where a CNN anchor was interviewing a shaven-headed Black man in glasses. The crawl read:

RACE FOR THE WHITE HOUSE

MAN LABELED "MY AFRICAN AMERICAN" SPEAKS OUT

GREGORY CHEADLE, MAN TRUMP POINTED OUT AS "MY AFRICAN AMERICAN . . ."

It took another beat for my brain to process the fact that Trump had said this shit days ago, and now we were already days forward in the news cycle, dealing with this fucking nut who had somehow become a celebrity while I was being chased around the country by feds. The CNN people were asking him how he felt about being called a sellout on Twitter.

"There's a gross inconsistency in the outrage that's directed toward me, instead of Mr. Trump," Cheadle began.

"My African American" had a voice that sounded like Richard Pryor's impersonation of a white nerd. The whole thing was pure minstrel theater, a network dragging this poor confused motherfucker up there for entertainment value. It was damn near impossible to process these weighty concepts while blitzed out of my gourd from all those Js of Blueberry.

Cheadle went on:

> It's inconsistent in that, on the one hand, they want to call me a sellout and an Uncle Tom, and that's fine. But the problem is, how can they look in the mirror, and call themselves the N-words, and all these other things . . .

Jesus! I thought. I changed the channel, surfing back and forth.

Finally I landed on a *Vice* investigation about a free-cannabis movement. The piece was called, "Wall Street's Legalization Gamble" and profiled a group called Responsible Indiana, which was trying to get a decriminalization initiative on that state's ballot.

I was so baked that it was hard to follow the story. A *Vice* story is always told by a correspondent who is twenty-seven years old and brandishing some combination of a) tattoos b) crossbody bags c) a lumbersexual beard or d) an androgynous haircut. I always felt with this outlet like I was shopping for clothes more than I was watching news. And they were never clothes I would buy, so that was confusing too.

In this episode I was paying attention, though. The reporter did have the beard—his name was Juha Maarten, and he was either Scandinavian or some new kind of Brooklyn hipster. But the locale wasn't exotic: it was Bloomington, Indiana.

The plot twist was that, instead of activists and ex-dealers pushing for legalization, Responsible Indiana was a consortium of private-equity titans and celebrities who'd invested in a vast chain of retail weed outlets they were planning on taking over the instant the vote passed.

Maarten, the reporter, explained:

> The ballot initiative would create a marijuana oversight board and allow for 800 retailers . . . The state has fewer Dunkin' Donuts shops . . . All trade would come out of just a dozen in-state farms, transforming a group of financiers and celebrities into a marijuana monopoly, virtually overnight.

Vice cut to a group shot of the Responsible Indiana bigwigs up on a stage at the IU campus, answering questions at what looked like a town hall. I had to blink to pick out the familiar faces.

Was that former NBA star World B. Free? Hell yes, it was. And who the fuck was he sitting next to? Was that *reality star Nick Lachey*?

Now I was tripping. It was bad enough that one reality star might be president, but now an Urban Outfitters version of *60 Minutes* was telling me my business—the one I'd shed blood, sweat, and tears over for nearly two decades, for which I'd risked my life and freedom—was about to be taken over by a fucking human V-neck sweater, reality-husband/boyband-star fuckhead like Nick Lachey?

Nah, no fucking way! Can't be. But then I listened to Lachey answer a question:

"Folks, passage of this proposal will result in much-needed economic development opportunities across Indiana. It will update the state's position on marijuana in a smart and safe way, and that's the important thing . . . What's that?"

Someone was asking Lachey a question.

"Excuse me?"

"Don't you live in L.A.? Why are you in Indiana?"

"Well, I can't stay in L.A. all the time. It's the weather. Sometimes, *98 degrees* is just too hot!"

Talk about corny. The crowd cheered. I felt sick. What the fuck is wrong with people?

I squinted in the background and I could see that the panelists—who also included a hotshot fashion magnate from L.A. washed-up-looking ex-drummer from a Christian heavy metal band—were speaking in front of a big, green-colored, printed backdrop.

It was like the backdrops you'd see at a presidential press conference, or an NFL coach's confab, where it looks like wallpaper: alternating logos for the organization and the corporate sponsor. Only instead of:

NEW YORK GIANTS Toyota—"Let's Go Places!" NEW YORK GIANTS Toyota—"Let's Go Places!" NEW YORK GIANTS Toyota—"Let's Go Places!"

It read:

RESPONSIBLE INDIANA Statement Partners Veridian Capital Management RESPONSIBLE INDIANA Statement Partners Veridian Capital Management RESPONSIBLE INDIANA Statement Partners Veridian Capital Management.

I snapped awake. These were the same companies Josh had been yachting with!

How had I not heard about this, I wondered? Upon consideration, it made sense. I'd been out of Indiana for a while, ever since Malik and I broke off ties over that fucked-up shipment a while back.

As I recalled this, I could vaguely hear the *Vice* reporter explaining that Responsible Indiana had already bought a dozen farms.

"The group is expected to enter into contracts worth $60 million annually," the narrator said, as the camera panned across the IU town hall.

As the camera moved, I caught an image. I saw it just for a second, but it changed my life.

Standing at the rear of the stage, behind the rope line, in what looked like a thousand-dollar gray suit with matching white silk handkerchief—surrounded by a group of other men in thousand-dollar gray suits with matching white silk handkerchiefs—was a familiar face.

Vihaan!

I almost had a heart attack. Outside of his work for me, I had never seen that fucking idiot dressed in anything fancier than a *Star Trek* T-shirt. How could he be wearing a suit? Who told him how to tie a tie? And what the hell was he doing there?

In an instant, the chambers of my mind tumbled one over the other, like dominoes. It all became clear. I remembered that Malik and I had gotten fucked up over a shipment I'd sent him years ago, but mysteriously never arrived.

That shipment had come to me by way of Vihaan, who had been late crossing the border at Windsor. Suddenly I remembered the story about the spilled coffee, and the Buffalo Bills Zubaz pants he'd been wearing when he delivered me the suitcase.

I also remembered having to tell him, after I returned from a bad trip to Indy, to live off his fucking salary. He didn't take that well.

177

Could that have been the reason he snitched? No, I realized, it could not have been. I assumed his first piece of business was giving up the shipment to Malik. But that had to have been done before I fired him, not after.

The rest of it all made sense. Vihaan knew every one of the other folks in my network who'd been hit. We had worked so closely I didn't even think to make this connection. Also, it had been so long since I'd dealt with the motherfucker.

Everything else came into very clear focus. If he'd been informing all this time, he was helping the state wipe out the opposition to new groups like Responsible Indiana. Somewhere in that trade lay the logic behind the appearance of this living-with-his-parents, no-sex-having, no-money-making loser in this multi-million-dollar "consortium."

The only thing this dude had to offer was his dubious background as the weak-link courier in a genuinely illegal cannabis ring, chosen only for the disarming cluelessness of his appearance. Perhaps Vihaan would be pushed forward as the legit cannabis-world face of the group, the same role these Wall Street clowns wanted Josh to play in Cali.

I don't even know how long I sat on the couch after that, thinking. The TV somehow continued on, but I stopped watching. Hours passed, I think. By the time I snapped out of my funk, it was dark out. With effort I stood up, turned off the TV, and walked over to my window. I parted the curtains and peered out.

Brutus, across the street, was arguing with his woman. She had her back arched and was pointing in his face. He was raising his arm like he wanted to backhand her. A bad scene. Under normal circumstances, I'd have gone out and broken it up.

But I was too freaked out. I shut the drapes again, walked upstairs, and sparked up another few grams of the Blueberry. The room filled with smoke and the boulder was twice as big this time. I crawled under my covers, thinking about all the new shit until I passed out.

The next morning, on a burner phone, I hit the last number I had for Vihaan with a text:

Saw you on Vice last night. Nice suit, motherfucker.

Instantly, I saw the "typing awareness indicator" showing that my message had been received and a response was being considered.

I stared at it for a minute, heart beating. Then I heard the swooshing sound:

Sorry to hear about your cousin. You're next, bitch.

So now I knew.

*

Two days later, I was in Detroit. Surprise visit to Jerome, my dependable second. He was about to get a battlefield promotion.

"You sure about this, dog?"

"Yuh."

The financial deal was more than generous. Really, just symbolic. I would charge ten grand a month for as long as he stayed in business. In return, he'd get my connect and my whole book of contacts. Every distributor, every city, all of it.

The business was worth ten times that. But my thinking on all of this was changing. I wanted Jerome loyal and happy. I wanted him to want to make that payment. I wanted him feeling so guilty about the lowness of it, he'd pay me early.

Rule: *Always be willing to spend money for goodwill.* That went with the other rule I was obeying here: *Get your money and get out.*

The first rule. The main rule. The rule almost nobody in the business ever gets to say they followed.

I was on the verge of joining that elite club.

Jerome and I would have to go on a road tour. I'd have to introduce him to everyone he didn't know already, set him up with my cousin, set him up with Doug. I'd have to tell him everything he needed to take over.

Jerome knew Vihaan. In fact, I fleshed out that the two somehow had stayed in contact over the years, albeit rarely. Jerome disliked him a little less than me, but still joked about the guy.

We called him "Dotty"—bad joke, I know, but shit, you can't be PC all the time. Where I come from when you referred to Indian people you had to specify between Native Americans or people from India. We would ask, red dot or feather? Vihaan was from India, so he was red dot. That evolved into "Dotty."

I said: "One last thing. Don't fuck with Dotty."

"Why?"

"Just don't. Some strange shit is happening."

Jerome nodded.

"All right. Whatever you say, dog."

I took a long look at his apartment. Jerome was still plugged into the music business somehow. His place was filled with concert posters and memorabilia. He clearly entertained a lot and there were a few bottles and a lot of full ashtrays in there.

On his coffee table, I saw a little baggie of Molly powder.

Were I still his boss, I might get knee deep in his ass about that. But I was nobody now. Just a landlord. He could do what he wanted. It was a scary realization. But also liberating.

I was out.

15

Eat what you can.

LeBlanc called me with good news:

"I got Buddy off."

"You got the dash-cam footage? He didn't swerve like they said?"

"No, it's better than that. He did swerve. That cousin of yours had so much fucking blunt smoke in his car, he couldn't see. Nearly drove into an irrigation ditch, as a matter of fact."

"So they had probable cause?"

"No, they did not. They'd already lit up the strobe when he swerved. Matter of fact, that's why he swerved. They hit him with the siren, he freaked out, then lost the wheel for a second in his cigar-cloud. He was too high to remember this."

"Why did they stop him, then?"

"I think we know the real reason. But they originally said it was the swerve. When I saw the dashboard footage, they filed an amended report stating that their actual reason for pulling Huey over was a violation of section 307.075 of Missouri state law, which governs the color of taillights. Basically the law says lights on the back of your car have to be red, there has to be two of them, and they have to be visible from five hundred feet."

"So?"

"So they claim they couldn't see them from five hundred feet. The dash cam was inconclusive. I'm thinking, they've got us. That determination is all in the mind of the cop. You can't argue it. But . . ."

"But what?"

"Body cams, I love body cams!"

"Why?"

"These cops walk up to Buddy, one on the driver's side, one on the other, to the rear. The arresting officer actually remembers to ask Buddy to hit his brake pedal, to see if the lights work. This must be an old trick they run to justify stops, because they had it down.

"So Buddy hits the brakes. The cop looks back, his partner nods—yeah, the brake lights work."

"And?"

"And *then* he leans in and, according to the police report, he notices 'a strong odor of marijuana.' This supposedly is the PC for the search. They pop the trunk and find the pounds. Game over, right? Wrong. Thank you, Ruth Bader Ginsburg!"

"Why?"

"*Lopez v. US*, Huey. Case from just last year. Cops in Nebraska pulled over a car, coincidentally after it swerved on a highway. They ask the guy if they can have their dog sniff the vehicle. He says no. They do it anyway, and find meth in the car."

"Is that why he's swerving?"

"Sure. But the cops get unlucky. They file federal drug charges on meth-head, who draws a rookie federal public defender, a young woman named Ellie O'Neal. It's their bad luck that she clerked for a judge with a civil rights background—a guy named Jimmy Mannion, an Irishman, used to be house counsel for the NAACP, went to Syracuse with Joe Biden of all people. Also, we used to fuck. I mean Ellie and me, not me and Bannion. Or Biden. Anyway, I'm trying to say, it's just luck I knew all about this case. It was like Ellie's third real court case, so she actually gave a shit about it, which is terrible luck for law enforcement generally, and for any cop doing a routine traffic stop.

"After reviewing the file, Ellie appeals the fuck out of the meth case, arguing that the stop is a Fourth Amendment violation of her meth-head client's right to be free from unreasonable searches and seizures.

"District court denies. No surprise. She begs her bosses to let her keep going, and they're like: not on our dime.

"She's like 'Fuck it,' and appeals, in her spare time. She writes a million-page brief. Knowing her, she probably cited the the Federalist Papers. I remember this because she canceled a weekend in Chicago we had planned to write the thing. Anyway, she gets it before the Eighth Circuit and they *affirm*.

"That's like a rookie hitting a grand slam in the bottom of the ninth. Unbelievable.

"Now every traffic cop in the country is in a panic, because the ruling basically says you can't fuck with a guy on a traffic stop after you've answered the question you've stopped him to ask. They would eliminate about 90 percent of the arrests police make on the road.

"So they appeal the ruling and it goes all the way to Washington. Most litigators don't sniff the Supreme Court their whole lives, but Ellie makes it on her third case. And no senior litigator in her firm can take it from her, because she took it on as a hobby.

"Long story short, she argues the case and the Supremes affirm the lower court ruling. The crux of the case turns out to be a seven-minute delay between when the cops issued a warning for the swerve and when they brought the dogs out to sniff.

"The high court rules that the seven-minute pause is a '*de minimis* intrusion' on meth-head's personal liberty. Majority opinion written by Ginsburg rules that authority for a stop ends when the officers complete the 'mission' of the stop, and that they do not earn 'extra time to pursue unrelated criminal investigations.'"

"So?"

"So that's what cops did with Buddy. Or at least, it's what they said they did. According to the new ruling, the lead cop should have turned and walked right back to his car as soon as he confirmed the brake lights worked. Instead, he tests the brakes, then smells the marijuana. Allegedly.

"You get it? If he does it in the other order—if he smells the weed first, *then* asks Buddy to check his brake lights—your cousin is looking at ten years. I hit them with *Lopez* in the brief and got lucky with a judge who was at least slightly to the left of Hitler. The guy actually ruled on the law, and now, Buddy's out."

"Out? Like *out* out?"

"Yeah. I was worried the D.A. would come out with their real probable cause, which I'm sure is your Indian informant. But they didn't. Just dropped instead. Apparently your informant is worth more to them than Buddy's ten years. So they released your cousin today."

"And that's it?"

"Motherfucker, I just got a guy with a trunkful of pounds a total walk on an arcane Supreme Court case that had been law for about two whole weeks when your cousin was stopped. That's pulling a hundred-mile heater way over the seats. Remember how you thought I was all that for getting Tory Boyd five years for shooting someone in the head? The whole projects was talking about that, right? This was better by a mile."

"If you say so."

"Damn right. Anyway, expect to hear from Buddy. He wants to see you, make things right."

"Ed, I'm out."

"Out? Like *out*?"

I thought I heard slight disappointment at lost fees for a split second, but he rallied.

"Huh. Well, good luck with that. I mean it. Still, talk to your cousin."

"All right."

He hung up.

*

A few days later, Buddy flew to Oakland to see me. I not only had to break it to him that I was out, but that I wasn't leaving him the business.

He was upset at first, but deep down he knew what I did, that he wasn't ready yet to be the man. He still fucked up too often. Getting hit seemed to smarten him up, though.

When I met him at the airport he was dressed like a college kid, button-down shirt, slacks, and a new pair of Sperry three-eye rubber-sole shoes that looked like something white people wear on boats. His usual loud getup was gone.

I told him: "Jerome is the man now, but I owe you. I'll bless you. Meantime, come stay with me."

He got in the car. Buddy was the first human being who ever saw my house. He understood that it meant something, and I appreciated that.

"Thanks, cousin," he said, on the way.

Meanwhile, Jerome had moved out my way. Because the important connects were all in California, he couldn't stay in Detroit.

He got himself a nice spot, in Nob Hill in San Francisco. Bought himself a whole apartment full of brand-new furniture, which he was always posting on Instagram. That and other things. I was worried about my man Jerome.

When you have the money, one of the things that media tells you is to spend it. They show you in ad after ad: this is the way you're supposed to treat the money. Buy shit, show out. Also, live wild.

Jerome went from being a guy who kept it tight and maybe partied a bit on weekends to being someone who was flying all over and turning his social media accounts into a fucking amateur reality show.

I saw one video clip of him taglined San Diego, where he was surrounded by women and buying a bottle of Clase Azul Ultra tequila. That shit runs about $4,000 a bottle. Thanks to my connections, Jerome was doing just fine, but he was spending like an NBA star. Anyone who looked at that account would get interested real fast in where a guy like this made his money.

More than that, Jerome was picking up a faraway tone to his voice. When I called him, which wasn't often, he seemed distracted, like he had something on his mind. It wasn't my business to care anymore, but the instinct was still there, and something in his voice made me nervous.

I said on the phone: "Jerome, I got someone I want you to see. You remember my man in St. Louis?"

"Yeah."

"He needs a little work on the arm."

I expected more resistance to this, but instead I just heard, in a lazy voice, "Yeah."

"Yeah what?"

"Yeah, okay. Just come by, bruh."

"Where?"

"Here."

"Dude, where is here? Your house?"

"No, shit, not there. I mean, I'm in Oakland right now."

"What are you doing in Oakland?"

He didn't answer and instead just gave me an address in lower Fruitvale, a fucked-up neighborhood full of bando houses. What was he doing there?

Buddy and I went over. At first I thought the address was wrong because the place looked so fucked up. It was a three-decker house with a rear entrance for the top floor, and the stairs were covered in enough peeling paint to make confetti for two Super Bowl parades.

We got up there, shrugged, and knocked.

"Who?"

"Jerome, that you?"

"Yuh."

We went in. I froze. Jerome was laid out on a couch, watching ESPN or some shit. One look at him and I could see he was fucked up on something, not weed. Eyes glazed over, pinpricks for pupils. Jerome usually dressed sharp, but now he was just in jeans and a white tank, wedged in a couch full of cigarette holes, eyes half closed, zoning out. So softly we could barely hear him, he said:

"What's up?"

But that wasn't the bad thing. He wasn't alone. The place was filled with guys who looked like straight-up gangsters, all covered in tats up to their necks.

One guy sitting near him was just a fat dude with no shirt on. He wasn't muscular, just big and tatted. I wouldn't want to sit next to a guy like that for any reason, professional or otherwise.

There were five of them.

Who the hell were these guys? I'd never known Jerome to fuck with types like this. I knew he had some friends from Atlanta, and I was getting the feeling that maybe this was that crew. These guys were obviously from out of state, I could tell that much.

In the corner of the room, on a night table covered in empties and butts, laid a worn-looking pistol—just sitting there, not close enough to any of the five people in the room to obviously belong to any of them. Looked like a Glock .40. If one gun is visible, I knew there were probably two or three more that weren't.

I didn't like any of this. Typically, I didn't deal with street dudes. I didn't get close to them. And I didn't like fucking with guns.

But I had a job to do, hooking Buddy up. I played as if it was all okay. I said:

189

"Yo, what's the market looking like?"

"Good, man. I got connect with these outs, they're fucking competing with ins, and we making a killing on it."

"I can see that. What's the ticket?"

He quoted some numbers at me. I tried not to say anything, but they were not good numbers. Product that used to sell for $1,250 was now selling for $800, or even $700. Remember, this was a few years ago. Josh's predictions about the weed market were coming true, and would prove out even more soon enough. The price would drop to $500 within a year.

I didn't like the whole scene and quickly moved things along.

Look, I said, you know my cousin here, he's solid, I've worked with him forever. Did a year for me once. Can you hook him up?

"Yeah," Jerome said, nodding.

Without a word, Fat Shirtless got up, walked into another room, and came out with a duffel bag full of pounds. Stomach bouncing, he tossed the bag at Buddy, who caught it midair. The fat man then handed over a piece of paper with a phone number on it.

"Hit that shit when you ready."

"All right."

Just to make conversation, I said:

"How's everything else, man, all good?"

Buried in that question was another question, which was, *Where's my bread?* Jerome was late with my monthly payment, and I didn't want that to get to be a habit.

Without saying anything, without even being hostile about it, Jerome started pretend-complaining about our arrangement.

"You must love this shit, huh, Huey? I do all the work, and all you gotta do is collect the money."

In that moment I knew Jerome was headed for trouble. Rule: *Never count the next man's money.* That always fucks you up.

If you start thinking about what other people are making when you're already doing good, that's when you start making bad decisions.

Jerome lightened up after that, said he was joking, and actually got up from the couch to hand me my monthly envelope. He wasn't trying to be disrespectful. But he was in a bad place.

He and Buddy exchanged a few more niceties, then we started moving for the door. On the way out I suddenly remembered to ask a question.

"Hey, Jerome, you haven't been fucking with Dotty, have you?"

Eyes on the baseball game on TV, he answered without looking up.

"Who?"

"Dotty. Remember I told you not to fuck with him?"

"Oh, yeah. No, we don't do business or anything, but I might have talked to him once or twice."

My heart jumped.

"I wouldn't."

"Why?"

"I just wouldn't."

"All right, man."

We left.

*

We shipped Buddy's package back to St. Louis, and soon after my cousin went home. In my mind, I was out, but had some leisure ahead of me. I had money saved up, but I had a rule: *Never touch your savings.* It's an offshoot of *Don't get high on your own supply.*

You don't touch your operating capital, unless you're putting it to work. And I hadn't decided what I wanted to do with my money yet.

In the meantime, I thought, I could live on Jerome's envelopes, keep it low-key, maybe do a little traveling. Down the road, of course, I'd need to get real work. I had an idea that I might want to get back into activism.

Laila had something going on, a cannabis minority committee that was pushing legalization issues on the one hand, and lobbying to stop things like the felon ban on the other.

She'd mentioned the group to me last time I'd seen her at her shop, and I had the thought that maybe I'd come back and ask her for a job. Might even tell her my John Edwards story, who knew?

Activism seemed like a weird career choice, but pretty much *any* job at this point would be odd, especially since the salary would be mostly fictional to me. But I had to start getting ready to live like a real person: square job, square world.

I fucked around for two weeks or so, doing not much at all. I took one flight to New Orleans to see a girl, came back just in time to have another argument with Courtney. I moved back in with her for a few days, we fought, then I moved back to my place.

I was back home for about a day when I got a call from Buddy. He basically said he'd turned the package over, and was ready to pay out, but when he called the number Fat Shirtless had given him, Jerome wasn't there. All he got were other guys.

That didn't sound right. I called Jerome's number once, twice, got no answer.

Sent texts. Nothing.

Looked at his Instagram, and saw: nothing new for nine days. His last posts were from Seattle.

Finally I called the number Buddy had. I recognized the voice as Shirtless. It was low and impatient.

"Where's Jerome?"

"He's not here."

"Yeah, but where is he?"

There was a pause.

"He's not around. He's safe."

I felt a lump in my throat. That's what I used to say to people when one of mine got locked up, or was on the run. I'd say, "He's okay, he's fine," or, "Don't worry, he's safe."

That's also what people said when someone wasn't alive anymore.

Jerome from that day forward was missing. That was a mystery, and I would devote a lot of time in the next months trying to figure it out.

It also meant I was out of the landlord business. No more monthly envelopes for me.

I was now officially an ordinary American, who needed to work for a fucking living.

Now what?

16

Never run from the front.

I once knew a Black guy named Leslie Johnson. I met him in 2008, when I was working for that union campaign in Cincinnati, trying to convert Black voters on gay marriage.

As part of my outreach, they sent me to talk to the Hillary Clinton campaign, and I ended up face-to-face with Leslie.

Remember, this was 2008. Barack Obama was running. And it was after the South Carolina primary, when things got nasty, and Bill called Obama a "fairy tale." There was the additional swipe about Dr. King being a big part of getting civil rights laws passed, but "it took a president to get it done."

And then there was the whole thing about Obama losing support with "hard-working Americans, white Americans." And of course there was the past with the "superpredators" comment. For most Black people I knew then, it was just not okay to fuck with Hillary over Obama.

Black women got a pass, because Hillary is a woman. But a Black man in 2008 who was a Hillary supporter for the most part was either getting a big check or was confused.

Leslie was full-blown fucking confused.

We met in Mount Adams toward the convention, when the race was already over for the most part. Everyone who was anyone, especially a Black anyone, had already moved over to the Obama campaign. Not Leslie. He was hanging in there. We were all at a meeting about gay marriage, and I basically said, "What the fuck are you thinking, dude?"

And he said: "My political role model is Queen Elizabeth."

I stared back, openmouthed. I was like, okay, the dude ain't right.

Some years later, I got a call from another old friend of mine, a guy named James Collison, from college. James, too, had gone into politics, as an organizer in Southern California. It was early in the 2016 race and I guess he needed a job in politics, because he was working for Hillary.

When James told me that on the phone, he must have heard my facial reaction through the line, because he was like: "I know. I *know*."

So there was a certain stigma for Black men when it came to working for Hillary. It was a carryover from her race against Obama.

This is how low things got for me in 2016, when I left the drug business: I ended up working for Hillary.

*

By late August, Jerome was no longer answering his phone at all. When I called his people, they just kept telling me that he was okay, he was safe.

I kept checking his Instagram account. It never changed. No new entries. By the time two weeks had passed, I was convinced: he was either dead or locked up.

When I really started to get concerned was when I got a text out of the blue:

Sorry to hear about your boy Jerome. But you know he was with the alphabets the whole time

My heart sank at this. I knew it wasn't true—if Jerome had been snitching, I'd be behind bars already.

I texted back: *Who the fuck is this?*

Of course, I knew who it was. And he knew that I knew.

You know who it is you fucking coon I can't wait to rearrange your face

The only person dumb enough to use that term, who'd ever used that term in front of me, was Vihaan. A range of questions now popped into my head. First of all, how did he know my new number? I'd changed it repeatedly since my near-miss with the DEA.

Second, why was he fucking with me? To what end? The man was about to become the weed king of Indiana with Nick Lachey. He didn't have anything better to do?

He acted like he knew everything about me, but he clearly didn't. The only reason I say that is because if he knew how tough the sledding was for me that summer, he'd have been rubbing it in. But he wasn't. He had no idea.

With Jerome out, I wasn't getting my ten bills every month. And I wasn't about to dip into my pension already.

So I went to work, with Laila's cannabis minority committee. Our idea was to leverage the interest in that year's presidential race into cannabis activism, use it to help protect the farmers and the dealers.

Before I knew it, though, we were getting our check from Hillary. Out in the workforce for ten minutes, and I had Leslie Johnson's job.

I know, *I know.*

We got the contract after an initial meeting with American Priorities, the main Clinton super PAC. If you know how political spending works, it's basically a sham. There's an old system for show, where campaigns raise money in limited amounts from individuals. Those donations go directly to campaigns.

The real money system involves the so-called "independent expenditure" committees, the super PACs. They raise unlimited sums of money from basically anywhere, and can campaign for or against any candidate as much as they want. They just technically can't coordinate directly with campaigns, although of course they do.

Before Laila and I had our meeting with American Priorities, we looked up the donors. They were mostly all hedge funds, the ones you'd expect, like Soros Fund Management. But about halfway down the list you could see other names:

Statement Partners

Archer Daniels Midland

Veridian Capital Management

We didn't jump to conclusions. We figured: maybe they just don't like Trump. We rationalized that it was just dumb money, donated to the Democrat, to do what they want with it.

Still, we were wary.

We had the meeting. To deal with us, American Priorities sent a dude named Yail Tennyson. I knew from my 2008 experience that the aides who work on Clinton campaigns all look like Robby Mook: like minor birds of prey in glasses.

They also all behave like Mook: officious little twerps who act like they're carrying the Secret to the Universe in their briefcases and constantly interrupt you in meetings to correct you on tangential misconceptions you might have about their candidate, like that you don't like her.

Tennyson looked just like Mook. In fact, I wouldn't have been able to separate them in a police lineup. He showed up for a meeting at Laila's skate shop/café jacketless, but in the standard gingham-and-tie getup. He took a seat inside with faintly detectable hesitation, looking like he might have preferred to put down one of those sanitary toilet seat covers first.

"I'll have a water," he said to the waitress. Laila frowned.

We got down to business. Laila explained that we were willing to staff up and hit doors both in Oakland and throughout the Bay Area. But we wanted to know what they were offering on cannabis.

"Our position is that we need more research."

Laila and I glanced at each other. I said:

"More research? Research on what? People been smoking weed for like fifty thousand years."

Yail received his water, sipped it, and nodded back at the waitress, as if to say, *Good water!* Then looked back at me.

"Our position is that there's great anecdotal evidence that marijuana can be beneficial to people who are experiencing great pain. We refer specifically to people with cancer or other chronic diseases. But because this is merely anecdotal evidence, we need to do more research. We're committed to funding that research."

I was ready for this conversation and said: "But there are countless studies here and abroad already showing medicinal benefits of cannabinoids."

"Well, we dispute the legitimacy of some of those studies. Not discounting them, but we'd like to recheck," Tennyson said. "I can tell you one thing we're very excited about, and that's a cannabis-based drug called Transdiolex. There is no intoxicating effect, but it looks like it has a bright future as a treatment of severe childhood epilepsy and Lennox-Gastaut syndrome."

"Lennox-Gastaut syndrome. What the fuck is that?"

"It's another severe epileptic disorder. We think cannabis has a bright future as a treatment. In any case, we just think it needs more investigation. You can see Secretary Clinton's appearance on the Jimmy Kimmel show where she spoke with great sympathy on the subject."

He handed over a pair of fact sheets that contained a picture of The Candidate seated with Jimmy Kimmel, laughing. Underneath the picture contained a headline:

CANNABIS: WE NEED TO KNOW MORE

Laila looked at the paper, then looked back at the guy.

"Look, if you want us knocking on doors to talk to people in our neighborhoods, we need something better than Len—what the fuck is it again?"

"Lennox-Gastaut syndrome."

"The people in our neighborhoods, they've been targeted for decades both as users and as dealers. So we need to know, is she going to just come out and support federal legalization?"

"Not at this time."

"Look, Yail," I said. "We've waited so long, and it's like, motherfuckers just wanna get it done, you understand? Maybe more research is a sensible thing, but nobody's trying to hear that shit. So I tell you how this will go, if I walk into a room full of cannabis people. I'll say: 'She wants to do more research because it'll help people with Lennox-Gastaut syndrome.' And that would pretty much be a non-starter for a lot of people, because—"

"I don't think you understand the Secretary's position on this issue. I think if you explain it differently, your people will understand. There's a lot of exciting research going on. If you sell it to them that way, they'll of course understand the wisdom of waiting just a little longer."

I didn't like being interrupted and considered fucking him up, off G.P. But I remembered that I was now dealing with a different professional dynamic, and just said:

"Can we at least say that she's not in favor of throwing people in jail for getting high?"

He paused and thought. The answer, clearly, was *not really*.

"We're in favor of moving toward a legalization scenario."

"If you're in favor of moving toward it, why aren't you in favor of getting all the way there?"

"We're in favor of moving toward it, pending further research."

"We're going in circles."

"What you can say is, we're willing to remove the drug from Schedule 1, which is exciting. We now concede that there may be accepted uses for the plant and do not necessarily classify it as having the high potential for abuse."

We went back and forth for a while, and before long Yail was Yail-splaining to us how much worse Trump would be for people of color, and how we should emphasize this because, "What did we have to lose?" We ended up emphasizing that we had an ability to mobilize Black voters and possibly also cannabis activists. It turned into a straight business deal, money for movement. We got a check and hit the streets. This was pretty much the opposite of what I had been doing for the union or even for Barack Obama.

Within a week or so, Laila had organized a meet with a bunch of minority cannabis activists. It wasn't a huge group, but some of the people fighting the felon law were there, along with some legalization advocates who had some outreach capability, and even just some plain old dealers, people I knew.

Reader, I sat in front of this crowd of good people, and preached the gospel of pragmatism. I did my best, but I didn't feel the love. A burly grower and dealer we called BK stood up and frowned.

"Let me get this straight. They don't want to talk legalization. How about decriminalization?"

I shook my head.

"Huey, what the fuck? What exactly do we get?"

"Listen. At the end of the day she's who we got. And we can have a seat at the table, or we can not. Understand, if we aren't at the table, than we are on the table. We can organize ourselves, and say, 'We helped get you here.' Do that, and maybe in the end we can make a list of demands to hold her accountable."

"Four years from now?"

"Yeah."

"Shee-et."

"Look, if we don't stand with her, you know what the alternative is? You know who the fuck Jeff Sessions is? This guy actually said he liked the KKK *until* he found out they smoked weed. That's who the fuck we're dealing with on the other side. They like the Klan better than pot. Process that shit."

"Yeah, but . . . well, fuck, you're right, that's bad."

"So that's where we are. That's the deal."

At the end of the meeting, everyone present ultimately agreed to vote, and also to encourage their people to vote. But they walked out with heads down, looking like they were headed to the dentist's office.

I met with Josh and Jay and a huge, mostly-white group from the Cultivators' Association too.

I had mixed feelings in this crowd. When I first learned about the Trump campaign, my feeling, as a Black man, was this: "They're never going to take jobs from white people."

So I'd go into meetings with white farmers, and in my head, I'd be thinking:

"If Trump wins or if Trump don't, y'all will be okay. You guys will still be able to grow your product guaranteed. But he's got a guy who's saying he likes the KKK more than he likes people who are down with cannabis, and shit, that makes me scared for my people right now. It makes me scared for you."

I'd say something like that. And I'd mean it, too. For anybody that would even say the same sentence, *I like the KKK more than whatever*, that's a problem.

It's one thing to ask: "What's better, the KKK or the Nazis?" You can imagine getting high enough to have that conversation.

But liking the KKK more than weed smokers? Get the fuck outta here.

So I'd lay a rap like that on the farmers, just to try to scare them. And some of them were hardcore, in-the-hills white folk, and to be honest, I didn't want to know their political views on everything. But I hoped they would be scared just on the weed level alone to get out and vote.

When I met with Josh and his people, he came up to me after and said, "Huey, there are easier things to sell than Hillary Clinton, I can tell you that much."

"I remember."

"What the hell happened? Everything felt so right just a couple of years ago. Huey, my biggest problem, every year, was figuring out which foreign country had the best beaches and prettiest girls." He shook his head. "I guess they can fuck up anything in this country."

I had a bit of a tough time sympathizing with Josh. His version of how hard life was going to be was that it would be sad for a few years. But seeing the look on his face on the way out of the meeting didn't fill me with confidence.

I must have repeated scenes like this fifty times between August and November. And every meeting ended the same, with people leaving agreeing to hit the polls and organize. But they always looked like they were passing kidney stones when they left.

On election night, I remember holing up in my Oakland apartment, alone, watching the returns and just shaking my head.

When they called it for Trump, I was hit with a flash of insight. I'd run track my whole life as a kid. One of the first things you learn: it's hard to run a race from the front.

In the front, you often don't know how hard you need to run, or even where you need to be on the track in order to box out the person running behind you. If I'm running in front, the quickest way for me to get from point A to point B is to be as close to the inside of the lane as possible.

But if there is a person behind getting ready to pass, you know you need to move over and maybe even bring your arms up to box them out.

Hillary and her crew of interrupting know-it-all fuckheads weren't paying attention. They ran as front-runners. Their only argument was inevitability. But inevitability don't make the heart beat.

You've gotta give people something—inspiration, fear, something—to get them to fight through their fatigue down that last stretch of track.

Never run from the front became one of my rules.

A few weeks after the election I sat down and tried to process what had happened to my life. I'd been able to cope in an America with a thriving underground, with margins big enough to accommodate a gently illegal business like mine.

Now the margins were disappearing. Life inside the lines in America didn't look so hot. Would there even be a place for me there? How many moves did I have left?

17

No guns, but keep shooters: Part II.

You could just barely hear it when the hotel key card beeped and the man entered. I knew the brand of door: ETO custom two-panel models, featuring quiet hinges and "ample sound-proofing." A staple of Marriotts all over the country.

Vihaan was backlit in the doorway, a silhouette. He stood for a moment, sliding his key card back in his wallet and fumbling with a briefcase. Made me laugh to see him decked in a dress suit. It fit that overgrown bellhop like scuba gear on a zebra.

He walked in and turned the lights on. There were eight of us.

"What's good, porky?" I said. "Have a seat."

The texts had been coming for months. Weird shit, pointless. Just *fuck you* at three in the morning. *Your bitch Courtney goin down too they got her ugly ass on conspiracy* was another late-nighter. There were long rants, calling me a coon and worse. Lots of talk about snitching that would have interested a shrink. The boy had problems in the head.

I didn't answer. Just thought about it. And started to track him online. When I saw he was going to be a panelist at an Oakland cannabis conference, I thought it was too good to be true. You're coming to *my* town after all that? Say no more. It's on.

I hit Buddy on Wickr and told him, "You got youngins tryin' to eat? I got some shit to sort out."

Buddy had left Missouri. He was in my neck of the woods now. With Jerome missing, he was working some of my old plugs, doing some light work with old outta-town buyers of mine. It was my way of looking out.

He followed the rules and never carried a gun. But shooters, he knew. Oakland shooters. Eighteen-, nineteen-year-old boys, too young to give a fuck. Like the type to catch a body because someone smudged their Pumps by mistake.

It wasn't hard to guess where Vihaan would stay. The conference was at the hotel. Wasn't hard to get in, either. For years, I had been giving the hotel staff points on deals they arranged with buyers that came in from out of town.

"Close the fucking door."

I thought about having someone in the hallway, but decided not to bother. Why pay for extra muscle? I knew Vihaan. He's a bitch. He'd sit the fuck down when told.

He sat down.

One of Buddy's goons stepped forward. The kid was named Francis, a Jamaican, reminded me a lot of Ro. Built and crazy. Like Ro, he probably had bodies on him.

That made the role we picked out for him funnier. Sound man.

"Huey, what the fuck, man—"

Francis walked up to where Vihaan sat—in the extrawide "chair and a half" that was another staple of the chain—and stole him hard enough that his pussy came off the leather.

"Shut the fuck up."

I nodded to Francis, who leaned over to peer at Vihaan's mashed face with professional curiosity, like a dentist checking to see if he'd set a crown right. Then he reached into his jacket and pulled out a roll of black electrical tape.

Vihaan saw that and started hyperventilating. Francis shook his head at him.

"Relax, motherfucker."

He took the tape and tore off a few short strips. Then he brought out a little TV microphone, one of those things you clip on a suit lapel upside-down, with a cord leading to a wireless transmitter you stick in your pocket.

Francis clipped the mic on and taped the cord on the inside of Vihaan's lapel like a pro. Then he handed him the metal UHF bodypack.

"Put it in your inside pocket, or your pants."

Vihaan looked up at him in terror, then meekly stuck the pack in his inside pocket.

"Now," I said, "we're gonna talk."

Buddy worked the camera. The rest of the crew sat behind the shot, in chairs or on the second double bed. They acted like part of a film crew, but they were carrying guns or baseball bats instead of boom mics.

"Huey, I'm gonna yell."

"Try me if you want to."

He thought about that, and didn't scream. He was stupid like that, always talking instead of doing. Had he just yelled for help, we'd have had a problem.

"Now, I want to know it all. If I don't hear what I want to hear, this won't end well, understand?"

I nodded to Buddy, who hit record. The little red light came on.

Vihaan peered side to side, like a kindergartener who didn't know the answer when asked two plus two. For a minute I thought he wasn't going to say anything at all. Then, in a flash, he was babbling.

Just as I thought, it all started in Windsor all those years ago. He got popped at the Canada-U.S. border. The way he told the story, the part about spilling coffee on his crotch was actually true!

It happened when the Customs officer came up to the driver's-side window. The guy was only coming to tell him he had bird shit on his door handle, but Vihaan was so scared the feds were onto him, he spilled scalding hot coffee on his dick and started freaking out.

He told the rest of the story so fast that I could barely understand it. But the essence was that Customs people ended up helping him out of the car, and in the course of friendly small-talk they asked him his fucking *name* and he forgot it. Within about two seconds they were searching the trunk and finding my packs.

They brought him into a room with gray-painted concrete walls—he remembered the gray paint, but not the name of the agent—and reading between the lines of his frenzied story, he offered up everyone he knew right there on the spot. They gave him a deal, sent him to meet me, and he was working for them from that day.

They tested him by hitting that big load Vihaan had hauled over that was supposed to go to Malik in Indianapolis. I never got an explanation why they didn't make an arrest with that.

Another explanation, I guess, is that they did arrest Malik's runner, and I just don't know about it. That might explain Malik's boy Blac pulling a pistol on me, and not paying that other debt. Maybe they thought I'd snitched.

Who the fuck knew?

All I knew was, that day changed my life. The load they hit was one I'd taken on credit from Kermit. That ended Canada for me. California turned out to be just as good. But California was changing, and I went with the change.

I think we'll look back at those years, the Obama years ironically, as the last golden age for people like me. When weed illegal but tolerated, it was really just another big American industry, with slightly different risks.

Airlines worried about crashes. Car companies worried about recalls. People like me worried about lost packages and maybe a little jail time.

But in each arena, it was great money. Easy money. I had a good run as a CEO in the last heyday of weed, and it ended because some dipshit kid from Cincinnati spilled coffee on his nuts. Go figure.

Anyway, back in the hotel room:

Vihaan's story got worse. I had to piece it together, because he seemed too dumb to pick up on it, but the feds must not have had a real informant above street level anywhere in the weed world, because they kept throwing money at him.

As he told it, from that day in Windsor, they showered him with snitch checks and arranged meets with celebrities and bankers and all sorts of people. I think because they wanted eyes on the emerging legalization movement too.

Maybe the point of that was just to snitch people like me out of the business, keep the old dealers away from the coming pot of gold. If so, I had to admit, it worked. They didn't get me, but they scared the dogshit out of me.

I could live with that. I *am* living with that. But I wasn't about to let this nut-burned, no-account punk cash in if I couldn't.

I gave him a few instructions and told him to speak slowly and clearly into the camera. He gulped and said:

"I, Vihaan Majeshwari, have been working for the Drug Enforcement Agency since 2009. I have told federal agents about illegal marijuana sales in Baltimore, Tallahassee, Indianapolis, New Orleans, St. Louis, Washington, New York, Oakland, Los Angeles, Cincinnati, and Cleveland."

He paused, looked around in despair, then went on:

"If you've bought tree off me, Vihaan, I've probably told police about it. They may even have tapes of our conversations. I am also informing on all my new partners in the legal cannabis business, and basically everything I've said in public, at conferences, and to the media has been what the feds wanted me to say."

I nodded to Buddy. He turned the camera off, and started downloading shit from one machine to another. I turned back to Vihaan.

"What're your iPhone and Instagram passwords?"

The startled look in his eyes told me that until that moment, he thought I was just going to keep the tape as insurance. Now he knew: not a chance! I saw his mind working slowly now.

"But Huey—come on, man, they'll fucking kill me. You know some of these people!"

"Dog. The passwords."

He heaved back and forth, rolled his eyes, and began hyperventilating again. I didn't ask him to, but Francis rocked his ass again, I think just out of impatience. He started to snot and whimper, rubbed his jaw, then whispered something real quiet.

"What?"

I leaned over. He whispered again.

We all burst out laughing. I typed in *1-2-3-4* to open the phone, then BABYDONG for his Instagram account.

"Wow, nice pictures. Is that your girlfriend?"

It was a cheap shot, but he'd been threatening Courtney, so I felt it was okay.

"Huey, please, man."

I nodded to Buddy. He sent something to a burner phone, and from the burner I sent a text to Vihaan. I punched in a few buttons, then showed Vihaan a black screen with the little "play" triangle in the middle. Then, with great fanfare, hit SHARE.

I looked back at him: "Get the fuck outta here."

"But this is my room!"

"You're right."

I looked down at his Instagram page, typed in ASK FOR ME AT THE FRONT DESK AT THE OAKLAND MARRIOTT, and hit SHARE again.

Vihaan gulped again, then looked up first at me, then at the others in the room.

"Go get the fuck out, bitch."

"Can I have my phone?"

"You can't be serious. I haven't had a chance to read everything in it yet."

He got up from the chair-and-a-half and ran out the door.

We all left a minute or two later, took separate cars home. Buddy was driving a new Escalade. He asked:

"What'd you actually upload?"

"Just some Notorious B.I.G."

I never actually circulated the video. But just knowing I had it sent Vihaan into hiding. Never heard from him again, never saw him again, never saw his name on a conference or anywhere online. He's probably backing bar again, in someplace like Cozumel.

Months later I called Responsible Indiana, out of curiosity, and asked for "Mister Maheshwari." The office assistant took on a strange tone at the sound of his name, then put me on hold.

Before I knew it, a familiar-sounding voice was on the line. Was that Nick Lachey? I laughed and almost inquired, but didn't bother in the end. Just asked: "Where's Vihaan?"

"He doesn't work here anymore."

"Gosh. There's nothing wrong, is there?"

"Oh, no. We talked to his family recently. He's fine."

"Fine, huh?"

"Yeah," the voice said. "He's safe."

*

I'm out now, for real. Haven't made a move in years. I dabble in politics and some other things. But I won't lie, I think about going back. America is hard and easy money tempts. But the game is just about done for people like me.

We live in a new era. I see it all around me here in the Bay Area. Technology, computers, businesses of scale. Eyes and ears on everything. No more corner bookstores: the game is about being the world's only bookstore. The new CEOs, in tech or in tree, are about monopoly. They want to own the whole world and force you to pay rent no matter where you stand. Where's the honor in that?

There was honor in hustling. I fought cops and competitors to make my pay, coaxing a beautiful thing out of the ground and bringing it to your door.

I didn't want it all. Just everything I had coming.

Someday, we'll miss the years when that was enough.

MATT TAIBBI is a contributing editor for *Rolling Stone* and winner of the 2008 National Magazine Award for columns and commentary. His most recent book is *Hate Inc.: Why Today's Media Makes Us Despise One Another.* He's also the author of *I Can't Breathe: A Killing on Bay Street*, about the infamous killing of Eric Garner by New York City police officers, *Insane Clown President, The Divide, Griftopia,* and *The Great Derangement.*

REGGIE HARRIS is the co-founder of Hyphae Labs, which is leading the industry in psychedelic mushroom potency testing, and the creator of Oakland Hyphae, which hosted the Psilocybin Cup and The Oakland Psychedelic Conference. He has over 10 years of domestic experience in the US cannabis industry, is a member of the Advisory Board for Decriminalize Nature, and is active and passionate in The Movement for Black Lives and an abolition of the police state.

CPSIA information can be obtained
at www.ICGtesting.com
Printed in the USA
JSHW041437270822
29836JS00001B/1